Library of
Davidson College

**JOHNSON REPRINT CORPORATION**
NEW YORK & LONDON
**1973**

*Library of Congress Cataloging in Publication Data:*

Vincent, Patrick R.
  The Jeu de saint Nicolas of Jean Bodel of Arras.

  Original ed. issued as v. 49 of the Johns Hopkins studies in Romance literatures and languages.
    Originally presented as the author's thesis, Johns Hopkins University.
    Bibliography: p.
    1. Bodel, Jean, 12th cent. Le jeu de Saint Nicolas. I. Title.
  II. Series: The Johns Hopkins studies in Romance literatures and languages, v. 49.
  [PQ1346.N52V5   1973]         842'.1        72-12563
  ISBN 0-384-64610-7

Reprinted from an original copy in the collection of Columbia University Libraries
First reprinting 1973, all rights reserved
Johnson Reprint Corporation, 111 Fifth Avenue, New York, New York 10003
Printed in the United States of America

THE JOHNS HOPKINS STUDIES IN ROMANCE LITERATURES
AND LANGUAGES

VOLUME XLIX

# THE *JEU DE SAINT NICOLAS* OF JEAN BODEL OF ARRAS

# THE
# *JEU DE SAINT NICOLAS*
## OF
# JEAN BODEL OF ARRAS

*A Literary Analysis*

PATRICK R. VINCENT

*1954*
BALTIMORE · THE JOHNS HOPKINS PRESS

Copyright 1954, The Johns Hopkins Press. Distributed in Great Britain, India, and Pakistan by Geoffrey Cumberlege: Oxford University Press, London, Bombay, and Karachi. Printed in the U. S. A. by the J. H. Furst Company, Baltimore.

*Library of Congress Catalog Card No. 54-12727*

To

A. G. A. B.

## TABLE OF CONTENTS

| Chapter | | Page |
|---|---|---|
| | Introduction | xi |
| | Synopsis of the *Jeu de saint Nicolas* | xiii |
| I. | Critics of the *Jeu* | 3 |
| II. | The Prologue and the *Iconia* Legend | 15 |
| III. | Epic and Crusade | 40 |
| IV. | The Tavern | 66 |
| V. | Integration | 83 |
| VI. | Versification | 92 |
| VII. | St. Nicholas | 97 |
| | Bibliography | 105 |
| | Abbreviations | 109 |
| | Index | 111 |

# INTRODUCTION

Since the manuscript of the *Jeu de saint Nicolas* came to light at the end of the eighteenth century, editors and scholars' clarifying obscurities have contributed to present a clear, comprehensible text of immediate appeal to the reader of medieval French literature. Literary criticism, however, has not kept pace with this development, for although the *Jeu* has generally been adjudged the best French miracle play, the tendency has been to praise single features at the expense of the others. It has been seen now as a crusading, now as a realistic, low-life drama, and although more attention has been paid in this century to the hagiographical element, criticism has not progressed to the discernment of the unity embracing these component parts.

From a close analysis of the literary aspect of the *Jeu*, Bodel emerges as a skillful dramatist of considerable originality. In utilizing the essential material of a traditional saint's Life, but recasting and adding to it to present an "up to date" version of the legend in the colors and spirit of his contemporary world, he achieved, for all the apparent disparity and incongruity of its component parts, a work of transcendent unity, an artistic expression of the attitude of the common man of twelfth-century Arras towards the active and familiar Saint Nicholas.

This study was prepared as a dissertation in partial fulfillment of the requirements for the degree of Doctor of Philosophy at The Johns Hopkins University. The author wishes to record his deep sense of gratitude to Professor Leo Spitzer not only for directing the dissertation but also for the pleasure and profit of four years of stimulating instruction and sympathetic assistance of which this study is the fruit.

PATRICK R. VINCENT

*January, 1954*

## Synopsis of the *Jeu de saint Nicolas*

Prologue—The narrator (*preecieres*) announces that on this Eve of St. Nicholas the saint is to be honored with a play concerning one of his many miracles. He delivers a detailed summary of the play.

Scene I—The King of Africa is told by his messenger, Auberon, that a Christian army has invaded his territory. Outraged, he reviles the idol of his god Tervagant, but soon imploring forgiveness, he seeks his help. From a sign the idol makes, he learns that he will defeat the Christians but will subsequently abandon his faith. The King orders the mobilization of his forces. II—The royal crier, Connart, proclaims the call to arms.

Scene III—The King dispatches Auberon to summon the distant peoples of his empire. IV—En route, Auberon stops at a tavern for wine. After quarreling with the Tavernkeeper and playing a game of dice with another customer, Cliquet, he resumes his journey. V—Auberon delivers the summons to the Emirs of Coine, Oliferne, Orkenie, and Outre le Sec Arbre. VI—Auberon reports the successful accomplishment of his mission to the King. VII—The Emirs join the King with armies and costly gifts.

Scene VIII—Informed by the Seneschal that his armies are ready, the King orders them into battle. IX—Seeing the Saracens approaching, the Christian knights resign themselves to a valiant death and are comforted by the Angel who promises them a place in Paradise. X—Wildly boasting, the Emirs attack, killing all the Christians but one, the Preudom, whom they discover praying to an image. XI—The Preudom prays to St. Nicholas for deliverance and the Angel urges him to trust in God and the saint.

Scene XII—Dragged before the King and questioned about the image, the Preudom says it is of St. Nicholas, savior of the distressed and great miracle worker. Treasure may be safely left to the care of the image. The King decides to test the power of the saint with his own treasure, holding the Preudom in jail meanwhile. XIII—Durant, the jailer, takes charge of the Preudom. XIV—The Angel assures the Preudom that St. Nicholas will help him and that the King and his barons will be converted to Christianity. XV—Assured of the safe custody of the Christian, the King orders his treasure to be left unguarded but for the image; this is to be publicly proclaimed. XVI—Connart cries the proclamation.

Scene XVII—Connart quarrels with another crier, Raoulet, who is crying the wine for the Tavernkeeper. XVIII—Pincedé, tempted by Raoulet's praise of the wine, enters the tavern. XIX—Old friends, Cliquet and Pincedé, drink on credit, to the disgust of Caignet, the potboy. XX—Rasoir, the third rogue, enters the tavern with the news of the King's treasure. Until the right time of night to steal the treasure arrives, the trio drink and dice, the Tavernkeeper, promised a share of the booty, extending their credit and tolerating their quarrelsome behavior. XXI—The thieves set out and steal the treasure unhindred. XXII—The Tavernkeeper welcomes the returning thieves. After an orgy of drinking and gambling they go to sleep, intending to share the stolen treasure the next day.

Scene XXIII—Roused by the Seneschal with news of the theft of the treasure, the King sends for the Preudom. XXIV—the Seneschal orders Durant to bring forth his prisoner. XXV—The King sentences the Preudom to death, but at his desperate entreaty grants him one more day to live. XXVI—the Preudom prays fervently to St. Nicholas for help. XXVII—The Angel tells the Preudom to be of good faith for St. Nicholas will soon help him.

Scene XXVIII—St. Nicholas arouses the thieves and orders them to replace the treasure. XXIX—The thieves express their terrified amazement. XXX—The Tavernkeeper, disclaiming all part in the theft, has Caignet eject the thieves from the tavern, retaining Cliquet's cape as a pledge for their debts. XXXI—The thieves replace the treasure and go their separate ways.

Scene XXXII—Finding the treasure restored, the King is overjoyed and again sends for the Preudom. XXXIII—Told by the King of the miracle, the Preudom thanks God and tells the King to offer himself to God and St. Nicholas. The King and the Seneschal renounce their faith, their example being followed by the Emirs, Orkenie alone proving unwilling but yielding to force. At the King's request the Seneschal overturns Tervagant. The Preudom, praising God, ends the play.

THE *JEU DE SAINT NICOLAS* OF
JEAN BODEL OF ARRAS

# CHAPTER I

### CRITICS OF THE *Jeu*

The *Jeu de saint Nicolas*,[1] composed by Jean Bodel,[2] jongleur and poet of Arras, between the years 1199 and 1201, and therefore by many years the first vernacular French miracle play extant,[3] was brought to the notice of the modern world from the sheltered obscurity of the library of the duc de la Vallière in 1779 by Pierre Jean-Baptiste le Grand d'Aussy.[4] This ardent, but in this instance critically undiscerning, collector of *fabliaux* and *contes* of the twelfth and thirteenth centuries adjudged Bodel's play a precious monument in the history of the theatre, basing this high opinion, however, solely on what he considered its value as evidence of the earliest shaping of a truly dramatic form in the evolution of the French theatre from, as he believed, the medieval *fabliau*, declaring it, indeed, void of any intrinsic literary interest or merit. So satisfied was he with his appreciation of the play that he found it unnecessary to reproduce from the manuscript more than the

---

[1] Editions: L.-J.-N. Monmerqué, *Mélanges publiés pour la Société des Bibliophiles français:* VII (Paris, 1834), pp. 3-84.

L.-J.-N. Monmerqué et F. Michel, *Théâtre français au moyen âge* (Paris, 1839), pp. 157-207 (with a translation).

G. Manz, *Li jus de saint Nicholas des Arrasers Jean Bodel. Text mit einer Untersuchung der Sprache und des Metrums des Stückes, nebst Anmerkungen und Glossar*, Heidelberg diss. (Erlangen, 1904); reviewed by A. Schulze, ZRP, XXX (1906), pp. 102-8, and by A. Guesnon, MA, XXI (1908), pp. 67-8.

A. Jeanroy, *Jean Bodel, trouvère artésien du XIIIe siècle: le Jeu de saint Nicolas*, CFMA (Paris, 1925); reviewed by A. Wallensköld, NM, XXVII (1926), p. 176; by A. Hilka, ZRP, XLVI (1926), p. 492; and by C. Brunel, BEC, LXXXVII (1926), pp. 407-8.

F. J. Warne, *Jean Bodel: le Jeu de saint Nicolas*, Blackwell's French Texts (Oxford, 1951); reviewed by G. Frank, RR, XLII (Dec. 1951), pp. 282-4; and by D. McMillan, MLR, XLVII (Apr. 1952), pp. 237-40.

[2] For the few details known about the life of Jean Bodel and for his literary activity, see O. Rohnstroem, *Etude sur Jean Bodel, thèse pour le doctorat* (Uppsala, 1900), pp. ix-xvi.

[3] *Le Miracle de Théophile* was written by Rutebeuf in or near 1265.

[4] Pierre Jean-Baptiste Le Grand d'Aussy, *Fabliaux ou contes du XIIe et du XIIIe siècle* (Paris, 1779), I, 336-47.

list of *dramatis personae* and the Prologue, translated into modern French, before asserting: " On ne peut nier que ce ne soit là un prologue tres distinct et l'annonce d'une véritable pièce dramatique. Cependant comme cette pièce n'est en grande partie que le miracle du prologue un peu étendu, qu'elle est très longue et encore plus ennuyeuse, je crois suffisant d'en donner un court extrait " (p. 341). The short extract is in the form of a brief summary of the opening scenes, the major part of the drama being dismissed as their easily anticipated development, not, however, without the comment: " A travers tous les défauts on y remarque beaucoup de mouvement et d'action et surtout un grand spectacle " (p. 345); but this is not to the credit of the author who is accorded the same disparaging treatment as his work: " Un poëte ignorant . . . comme il ne sait point l'art de faire disserter ses héros il les fait agir. Voyez dans Shakespeare quel fracas d'action " (p. 346).

As might be expected, Le Grand d'Aussy promptly stifled with his summary dismissal of the *Jeu de saint Nicolas* any interest or curiosity his discovery might have aroused, thereby delaying for many years a truer appreciation of its worth. For this he was inevitably, although almost sixty years later, taken to task by Onésime Le Roy,[5] who said of him: " Si ce laborieux explorateur s'était arrêté davantage sur tous les manuscrits qu'il voulait nous faire connaître il eût probablement remarqué d'abord le but du *Jeu de saint Nicolas*, bien dramatiquement exposé dès la fin de la première scène; il eût ensuite aperçu dans quelles circonstances mémorables, dans quel esprit religieux cet ouvrage a été composé et il n'eut point détourné si longtemps notre attention d'un aussi curieux monument " (p. 15).

For reasons vastly different from those of Le Grand d'Aussy did Le Roy praise Bodel's drama, describing it as " le premier monument dramatique dont puisse s'honorer la littérature française " (p. 15). He understood it as a reflection of the fierce crusading spirit which swept Europe and particularly France in the Middle Ages, as a deeply religious and fervently patriotic drama inspired by and artistically recording particular events of a glorious period in the history of France in her rôle of champion of Christendom against the Saracen. The particular events were the unsuccessful first crusade of Saint Louis which culminated in the glorious

---

[5] Onésime Le Roy, *Etudes sur les mystères* (Paris, 1837), pp. 13-32.

disaster of Mansoura in 1260, where fell so many of France's noble Knights, among them Robert, count of Artois (the *Crestïens nouviaus chevaliers* of the play) and the projected second expedition of Louis, the object of which was the conversion to Christianity of the king of Tunis. In short, in the *Jeu de saint Nicolas* is to be recognized the birth of French national tragedy (pp. iii-iv).

To substantiate this thesis it was necessary for Le Roy to dwell upon and exaggerate the crusading element at the expense of the hagiographical and realistic low-life elements which are scarcely consonant with the tone of epic grandeur with which Le Roy wished to invest the whole work. Although the subject of the play, the legend of St. Nicholas, according to this critic, is little more than a vehicle for a historical drama of the Crusades, appealing to the national fervor and Christian zeal of Bodel's contemporaries. The illustration of the powers of the saint is of much less consequence than the spectacle of the conversion of the king of Africa, the real object of the drama. The contribution of the scenes of Arras low life to the *Jeu* is minimized even more than that of the hagiographical element. These scenes occupy three-quarters of the drama, yet Le Roy considered them only insofar as they are essential to the development of the action of the crusading element. His interest in their inner character was limited to the brief remark that there is some poetry in the lines of Connart crying the tavern keeper's wine, but, far from making this a point of departure for a penetrating critical study, he dismissed this entire aspect of the *Jeu* with the implication of an incongruity better to be passed over without comment. There is an indication of the critical embarrassment felt by Le Roy when faced with the imposing bulk of these scenes of low realism in his uneasy explanation of the contrast of tones of lofty grandeur and less sublime gaiety. He suggests that a reconciling factor existed in the attitude of the Christian warrior to hardship and death: " Cette mort pour eux était loin d'être triste: aussi l'auteur va-t-il passer au ton le plus gai, du milieu de scènes qui seraient lugubres pour nous " (pp. 25-26 and note).

The next major contribution to the study of the *Jeu de saint Nicolas* came, after the lapse of almost another fifty years, from Petit de Julleville,[6] who did much to correct the biased view of

---

[6] L. Petit de Julleville, *Les Mystères* (Paris, 1880), I, 95-107.

Le Roy and to prepare the way for a more balanced understanding of the play. He himself was unable to achieve that understanding since, despite his unprejudiced approach and his attention to the multiplicity of interesting features of this drama, he was hampered partly by the obscurity of much of the dialogue but mostly by his determination to allow no personal enthusiasm to lead him into such gross errors of exaggeration as those of Le Roy. Consequently he curbed his enthusiasm too strongly and, remaining too literal and unimaginative in his appreciation of detail, he was unable to arrive at a moment of total comprehension. As a result, his study presents a series of accurate initial observations almost inevitably marred by subsequent deprecatory or contradictory comment.

As if about to discuss the significance of Bodel's use of the legend of St. Nicholas in the rôle of guardian of treasure, as a key to the appreciation of his *Jeu*, Petit de Julleville speaks of the popularity of the saint in Bodel's day, the importance of the occasion of his feast, the existence of the four Latin miracle plays of the Fleury manuscript, and the play of Hilarius, all with St. Nicholas for subject.[7] But, according to Petit de Julleville, to write a miracle play was not Bodel's inspiration. Evidently ordered to furnish a play for St. Nicholas' Eve, he merely utilized the idea he found in the other plays mentioned above in order to introduce material more to his liking: ". . . le miracle n'est plus qu'un prétexte à d'ingénieux développements" (I, 98). Bodel's real interest, we are told, lay first in moving the audience with allusions to the struggles of the Crusaders with the Saracens, certainly a heartfelt interest of his contemporaries, and then to amuse them with lively and realistic scenes of Arras as they knew it. This observation might have led to an insight into the integrity of Bodel's creation but it is not developed and this premature false conclusion is drawn: "On était ainsi tour à tour ému et réjoui.

---

[7] The Fleury manuscript, so called from its origin in the monastery of Fleury (also known as Saint Benoît-sur-Loire), is a collection of Latin liturgical plays of the early twelfth century. Four of these plays treat different legends of St. Nicholas. The text of the ten plays was published by Monmerqué, *Mélanges*, pp. 91-213. See Otto E. Albrecht, *Four Latin plays of St. Nicholas from the twelfth century Fleury play-book* (Philadelphia, 1935). Hilarius' play, *Ludus super iconia sancti Nicolai*, in Latin with French refrains, also of the early twelfth century, was first published by J. J. Champollion-Figeac, *Hilarii Versus et Ludi* (Paris, 1838).

Par quelle incohérence de moyens nous n'aurons pas besoin de le faire remarquer! Toute espèce d'unité est inconnue à Jean Bodel, et il use, avant Shakespeare, des plus grandes hardiesses de Shakespeare" (I, 98).

The crusading episode Petit de Julleville found admirable, equal to the best pages of the Roland and, dwelling upon its beauty, he makes the pronouncement: "Il y a là dans l'œuvre de Bodel des vers qu'on peut comparer aux plus beaux que le moyen âge ait écrits" (I, 99). He hastens to record his disagreement with Le Roy, neverthless, that the *Nicolas* is in any way *tragédie nationale*. He was correct, as subsequent research has shown,[8] in questioning the direct reflection or recording of the particular events of history his predecessor claimed to see in this episode but again he tends to detract from the value of his initial opinion by attributing Bodel's sublime poetic treatment of these scenes to caprice or chance. More satisfactory is his statement that, despite their beauty, they must not be considered as giving import to the whole play, because the popular scenes take up three quarters of it. This obvious but new statement introduces yet another opportunity to enquire effectively into the real nature of the drama but the very statement which gives most hope of such an enquiry also betrays Petit de Julleville's unawareness of the opportunity; speaking of Bodel he says: "Son vrai domaine est la réalité exacte et vivante, mais peu poétique" (I, 102). The scenes of Arras low life thus characterized, despite his echoing of Le Roy's comment on the poetry of the crying of the wine, Petit de Julleville is unable to integrate them into the drama. He is disturbed by the transposition of the action from the Saracen court to an Arras tavern which is somehow still in the Orient. Saracens are out of place in the tavern scenes ("Les Arabes ne boivent pas de vin"), which despite their undoubted popular appeal, are, he considers, far too long.

Stepping back, as it were, to view the play as a whole, Petit de Julleville concludes his study with little praise for Jean Bodel, but, in keeping with the contradictory nature of his criticism, with every indication at the outset of giving anything but adverse com-

---

[8] For the summary of opinions in the controversy over the chronology of Bodel's works and the establishing of the date of his death as in 1209 or 1210, which finally disproved the theory of the reflection in the *Jeu* of the events of St. Louis' crusade, see Rohnstroem, *Etude*, pp. x-xii.

ment: "Ce qui nous frappe avant tout dans le *Saint Nicolas* c'est l'originalité de l'œuvre. L'auteur nous a donné le premier, trois siècles et demi avant Shakespeare, six cents ans avant les Romantiques, je ne dis pas la théorie (en ce temps-là on ne faisait pas de théories littéraires) mais l'exemple du drame, tel que les modernes ont cru l'inventer vers 1827" (I, 104). In elaboration of this finding, Petit de Julleville indicates how Bodel anticipated the Romantics in all essentials. He fused the comic and the tragic, he treated national history and low life, he portrayed all classes and manners of characters, both human and divine, he felt no call to respect any unity of time or place. All this, however, is not to praise Bodel but to deflate the claims of the Romantics to originality. The violent juxtaposition of elevated and low themes seen in the *Jeu de saint Nicolas* was a bold and vigorous enterprise but, even if it were possible to carry out successfully, it was certainly not within the scope of Bodel, "poète sans génie et d'une âme commune" (I, 106).

Both Le Roy and Petit de Julleville were mainly concerned with a comprehensive study of the nature and development of the whole medieval French theatre and their shortcomings in respect of the one play under discussion must, therefore, be ascribed largely to the exigencies of this type of undertaking. An historical survey of this nature, concerned with tracing broad lines of development and presenting an overall view, must observe strict proportions and a certain economy in the treatment of detail and necessarily precludes intensive and exhaustive interpretation of individual works. When it fell to Otto Rohnstroem [9] to reopen the enquiry into the *Jeu de saint Nicolas*, his was the greater chance of arriving at a truer interpretation, for although his attention was not turned to this work alone, his study embraced only the works of Bodel and he was able, therefore, to pursue his investigation into the nature and literary merits of the play with a new thoroughness. His treatment of this miracle play marked a great step forward in the long history of its clarification and his views have been substantially adopted by subsequent readers.

The main feature of Rohnstroem's study and his greatest contribution to the modern appreciation of it was the rehabilitation of the saint's legend as the principal motif. This, we are made to

---

[9] Rohnstroem, *Etude*, pp. 41-70.

realize, is a genuine miracle play and the legend of the *Iconia sancti Nicolai* is not to be regarded as a mere pretext for a national tragedy, as Le Roy claimed, or for a more complex presentation of crusading and tavern scenes. It is, indeed, "le plus important des ouvrages français qui traitent de la vie ou des actions de ce saint" (p. 45).

One half of the study is devoted to what might be called the Nicholas background to Bodel's *Jeu*. Introductory sections deal with the historical and legendary Bishop of Myra, his cult as a saint in the West in the eleventh and twelfth centuries and its expression in the liturgical drama. The particular legend utilized by Jean Bodel is then given special consideration in the form of a comparison with the relevant passage in the *Legenda aurea* of Jacobus de Voragine,[10] which, although composed towards the end of the thirteenth century, reproduces legends current in Bodel's time, with the *Iconia*[11] miracle play from the Fleury manuscript, with Hilarius' *ludus*[12] and with the version of the same legend in the twelfth century *Vie de saint Nicolas*[13] of Wace. Allusions are also made to still other "Lives" both English and French. Rohnstroem's primary object is the establishing of a specific source of Bodel's drama, but in view of the close similarity of all the versions he discusses and the certainty of still others existing, so popular was this legend, he admits his inability to identify the model. Nevertheless, recalling Bodel's statement in the prologue: "Che nous content li voir disant/ Qu'en sa vie trouvons lisant . . . ," he elects the *Vie* of Wace as the probable source, basing this opinion upon the similarity of the two versions and on the literary reputation of Wace, whose works were no doubt familiar to the literary-minded people of Arras.

As Rohnstroem indicated, the Nicholas legend is the principal motif in Bodel's play as it was in the two earlier dramas and in Wace's poem. Bodel, however, developed and enriched it, considerably mitigating the uncouth and superstitious attitude towards the miracle shown by his predecessors, particularly Hilarius. From the earlier saint dramatically intervening in human affairs through

---

[10] *Jacobus a Voragine, Legenda aurea vulgo historia lombardica dicta,* ed. Th. Graesse (Dresden and Leipzig, 1846), pp. 22-29.

[11] For editions see below, Ch. II, note 15.

[12] For editions see below, Ch. II, note 14.

[13] For editions see below, Ch. II, note 11.

base fear of, or because of, his statue's being badly treated, there emerges the figure of a loftier saint impelled by a desire to save his true believer and not only saving him but bringing about the conversion of a whole people to Christianity.

In considering the crusading episode the most interesting literary feature of the *Jeu*, Rohnstroem is essentially in agreement with Le Roy and the more temperate Petit de Julleville. To their comments on its merits, however, he adds the observation that the germ of this element is discernible in many of the versions of the legend which place the miracle in a setting of Christian and Saracen conflict, at the same time avoiding the appearance of detracting from Bodel's inventive genius for, as he insists, the scene in its development must be seen as the author's own creation. As with the earlier critics, Bodel's inspiration for these crusading scenes is attributed to the spirit of his times, the all-pervading atmosphere of religious and martial excitement giving rise to and attendant upon excursions against the Saracen, but whereas Petit de Julleville implies merely a happy choice of subject on the part of Bodel, calculated to accord with contemporary interests, both Le Roy and Rohnstroem emphasize the more subjective nature of the author's expression. Rohnstroem, particularly, not only dwells upon the spirit of Western Europe at the time of the Fourth Crusade, born of the emotional shock of the fall of the Holy Land at Tiberias in 1187, increased by the stirring events of the Third Crusade with its brilliant figures of Richard Cœur de Lion and Saladin and fostered by Pope Innocent III through such spokesmen as Foulque de Neuilly, but also indicates the personal enthusiasm of Bodel himself for the proposed expedition to recover the lost shrines from the pagans, as it shown by his moving expression of regret, in his poem *Les Congés*, of being unable to fulfill his Crusader's vows because of leprosy. Nevertheless Rohnstroem is far from agreeing with Le Roy that the *Jeu de saint Nicolas* merits the appellation of "tragédie nationale." Such an extreme comparison cannot be made but, even so, his work has great merit: ". . . on est pourtant en droit de regarder la scène de la bataille dans le Jeu de saint Nicolas comme l'expression fidèle du courage chevaleresque et de l'ardeur religieuse de son temps: la forte impression que font ces quelques couplets malgré leur brièveté et leur sécheresse, tient à leur caractère à la fois sincère et noble, vigoureux et simple" (p. 63).

Following the lead of Petit de Julleville, Rohnstroem elaborates the observation that the pious and heroic scene of battle does not set the tone of the whole play. The principal motif of the miracle of St. Nicholas runs through a series of lively and grotesque scenes, generally lacking in poetry, although not without a certain dramatic power and brisk, natural dialogue, notable among them the Arras tavern scenes of drinking, gambling, and quarreling; these, we are told, interested author and audience the most and it is to them that the play owes its character. Again is raised the question of the plausibility of Bodel's fusion of East and West, of Africa and Arras: " Dans les scènes de la taverne, il faut voir sans doute des tableaux de la vie dans la joyeuse ville natale du poète: l'auteur qui place le sujet de sa pièce en Afrique, qui fait même quelque effort pour lui donner une couleur exotique, oublie, dans la peinture des trois buveurs, qu'il se trouve en Afrique et nous transporte subitement du pays des sauvages Sarrasins dans la riche ville du nord de la France" (p. 63). Rohnstroem fails, as did Petit de Julleville, to meet the challenge of the apparently violent clash of the exotic and local of which this strange geographical juxtaposition is the main illustration. He attempts to explain it away, yet at the same time noting specific efforts on the part of Bodel to give touches of an oriental background, by having recourse to the commonplace that medieval writers disregarded " local color " as, for instance, in the Chansons de Geste where Christian and Saracen are indistinguishable the one from the other both in appearance and general behavior. The inadequacy of this explanation is underlined in the well-conceived analysis of Bodel's character drawing to follow. Previously little attention had been paid to this aspect of the *Jeu*, Le Roy alone singling out the King of Africa for lively appreciation in order to emphasize the climax, as he saw it, of the conversion of the pagan enemy to Christianity, a capital aspect of his understanding of the *Jeu*. Now, all the major characters are discussed and each is shown to be well developed and invested with a distinct personality. There emerges from this, however, to contradict the assertion that the *Jeu* is barren of local color, the realization that the Saracen characters are at least adequately portrayed as such and are readily distinguishable from the others. This is particularly true of the king: " Par sa cruauté et son despotisme *le roi* est bien un monarque oriental " (p. 64).

Apart from the considerable literary merit he discerns in Bodel's miracle play Rohnstroem distinguishes "ses contributions précieuses à l'étude des mœurs et de la civilisation de son temps" (p. 68). The tavern scenes are described as rich in popular expressions and allusions to such details of medieval life as the selling of wine, the "eskievins de la cité" as opposed to the "homes de le vile," town criers and their duties, gambling habits and the frequent invocation of saints and mention of their legends in ordinary conversation. Such allusions are to be found not only in the tavern scenes but elsewhere throughout the play. The portrait of the jailer gives an insight into the fate of criminal offenders of that time and even the action which unfolds in Africa is reminiscent of local Arras and perhaps general French practices of the period, as, for example, the African king's relationship to his subjects which suggests feudal Europe, his attitude towards his god, Tervagant, in ornamenting his statue with gold, which recalls certain Christian practices of the Middle Ages; and his calling of his subjects to arms by means of a crier to proclaim his "ban" which particularly bears the mark of contemporary French civilization.

These allusions and details do indeed throw a valuable light upon the customs of Bodel's day but their divorce from the literary evaluation of the play would not seem to be justified. They are profuse enough to contribute considerably to the play's general character, providing not only touches of "local color" to satisfy our curiosity concerning the daily aspect of medieval life, but undoubtedly adding vastly to the appeal of the drama to the contemporary audience. Moreover, the appearance of these allusions in what are properly Saracen scenes to which, as Rohnstroem says, Bodel sought to give an exotic atmosphere, adds to and complicates the very feature so far unsatisfactorily approached, the close intermingling of the far exotic and near realistic elements which is so dominating.

Let it be said of Rohnstroem, however, in conclusion to this analysis of his criticism that he was aware of the potential significance, although not realized, of the *Jeu de saint Nicolas* in the history of the early French theatre: "En effet, la France aurait bien pu voir sortir du drame de Bodel un théâtre national. . . . Mais les auteurs de miracles et de mystères après Bodel ne furent pas à la hauteur de la grande mission que le trouvère d'Arras leur avait imposée par son ouvrage si plein de germes féconds et remarquable: sous leurs mains inhabiles, le genre vécut, comme les prisoniers de Durand, 'en mourant,' et la tragédie classique de la Renaissance, dans sa marche triomphale, ne trouva en France au XVI$^e$ siècle qu'une littérature dramatique presque morte" (p. 68).

Rohnstroem's view of the *Nicolas* has essentially been that of more recent scholars.[14] The prefaces to the most recent editions, those of Jeanroy and Warne, present the same pattern of discussion and adopt his conclusions, both noting the hagiographical motif and the appeal of the crusading scenes, dwelling most on the vividness of the realistic, low-life elements and characterization.

In this survey of the highlights of the critical appreciation of the *Jeu de saint Nicolas* from the date of its discovery to the present century, an attempt has been made to show that, although great progress has been made towards a worthy understanding of the first miracle play of France, the tendency has been and remains, to judge it on the merits of separate features, prominence being given in turn to the heroic, the realistic and the hagiographic elements as distinct component parts, with a notable absence of an attempt to present an underlying unity.[15] On the contrary,

[14] The opinions of critics before Rohnstroem seem to be based upon the findings of Petit de Julleville, although not without reminiscences of Le Roy. Thus, for example, Gaston Paris, *La littérature française au moyen âge* (Paris, 1888), pp. 239-241, stresses the double aspect of the *Jeu*, seen in the crusading scenes and the scenes of low life, discounting the hagiographical element almost entirely; Léon Clédat, *Rutebeuf* (Paris, 1891), p. 148, praises the crusading scenes but deplores the play as a whole: "Suivant le goût du temps, les scènes les plus relevées et les épisodes les plus vulgaires se succèdent dans ce drame touffu et maladroitement construit . . ."; Eugène Lintilhac, *Le théâtre sérieux du moyen âge* (Paris, 1904), pp. 248-258, was impressed by the crusading scenes which he saw, however, as only an hors d'œuvre to those of Arras low life, which despite a certain vivacity and witty dialogue, are "démesurées" and of only a documentary value. He, too, condemns what he calls "la bigarrure des tons": "Cette bigarrure est simplement l'effet d'une insouciance complète de l'unité d'impression chez notre trouvère; et si le disparate tourne parfois à un effet de contraste intéressant, il ne l'a pas fait exprès" (p. 258). See also Marius Sepet, *Origines catholiques du théâtre moderne* (Paris, 1901), pp. 177-201.

[15] An interesting exception to this might be claimed in the comment of Ida Del Valle de Paz, *La Leggenda di S. Nicola nella tradizione poetica medioevale in Francia* (Florence, 1921), pp. 96-107. Here, the *Jeu* is explained as an intensely lyrical work, not so much a miracle play as the

critics have expressed, as we have seen, varying degrees of embarrassment at the apparent irreconcilability of such disparate but closely interwoven elements. With the benefit of these critical studies, however, no matter how incomplete or biased they may be, and with all the advantages of the availability of a text clarified by a succession of scholarly enquiries it appears possible to approach the *Jeu* afresh and, by amending or extending previous literary criticisms, progress from an appreciation of particular features to a balanced, all-embracing view of its total inspiration.

---

record of the conflicting interests of an impressionable jongleur, addicted to the baser pleasures of life but not insensitive to higher spiritual calls. The contrasts and incongruities of the play are justified artistically (it is claimed) as accurate representations of the incongruities and contrasts of the emotions and interests of the author: ". . . e se da una parte riceviamo l'impressione dell' accozzo bizzarro dei toni più disparati, tutto viene a spiegare col suo sorriso un po' tormentato, la strana, complessa figura di Jean Bodel, pellegrino e gaudente, esaltato de misticismo in mezzo ai tracorsi della sua fragila umanità" (p. 107).

## CHAPTER II

### THE PROLOGUE AND THE *Iconia* LEGEND

>Nous volommes parler anuit
>De saint Nicolai, le confés,
>Qui tant biaus miracles a fais.   (vss. 4-6)[1]

Thus, having respectfully saluted his audience, does the *preecieres*, the narrator of the Prologue, introduce the subject of the play to follow. He then relates the particular legend of St. Nicholas to be presented. There was once (he narrates) a pagan king whose forces routed the invading army from a neighboring Christian country. After the battle there was dragged before him an old Christian survivor (the Preudom) who had been found praying to an image of St. Nicholas. Questioned about the image, the Preudom declared that the saint whose image this was would never abandon those who called upon him and, also, was such an excellent guardian that anything entrusted to him would increase. Holding the Christian captive, the King put his claim to the test, placing the image upon his unlocked treasure chests. When robbers stole the treasure the king condemned his prisoner to death but he was persuaded to delay the execution of sentence one more night, which time the Preudom spent in prayer to the saint. Mindful of his servant's plight, St. Nicholas appeared to the thieves and terrified them into returning the stolen treasure immediately, whereupon the King, impressed by the miraculous event, was converted to Christianity and his subjects with him. The Prologue concludes:

>Del miracle saint Nicolai
>Est chis jeus fais et estorés:
>Or nous faites pais, si l'orrés.   (vss. 112-114)

Accepting the definition of the miracle play as the dramatization of a legend setting forth the life or martyrdom or miracles of a saint,[2] even with the added limitation that by legend must

---

[1] The text of the *Jeu* quoted throughout this study is that of Warne's edition.

[2] J. M. Manly, " Literary Forms and the New Theory of the Origin of Species," *MP*, IV (1906-7), 577-595.

here be understood the non-Biblical accumulations about the names of hallowed and canonized persons in the Middle Ages,[3] it transpires from the Prologue that Jean Bodel conceived of his *Jeu* as a miracle play. In its character and quality as a miracle play, then, must be sought the key to its understanding and appreciation.

Despite the inability of even those critics whose attention is first drawn to the hagiographical motif, to achieve a satisfactorily comprehensive view of the *Jeu,* their point of departure—an enquiry into sources—is clearly the most practical since, the subject of the play being a well known and often treated legend of a highly popular saint, the problem of the poet's indebtedness to predecessors looms large in estimating his inventiveness and his originality in adapting to his own purpose the material he fell heir to. Bodel himself, through the *preecieres,* seems to acknowledge such an indebtedness, for on four occasions he makes what appear to be references to a specific written source:

> Che nous content li voir disant
> Qu'en sa vie trouvons lisant
> Que jadis fu uns rois paiiens. . . .   (vss. 7-10)

> Mais pour abregier le miracle,
> M'en passe outre, selonc l'escrit. . . .   (vss. 60-61)

> Mais issi le conte le lettre
> Qu'en se chartre le first remetre. . . .   (vss. 79-80)

> Signeur, che trouvons en le vie
> Del saint dont anuit est la veille. . . .   (vss. 104-105)

By comparing Bodel's version of this legend with other versions known to exist in his day, one might, then, expect to establish the source he appears to insist upon.

The wealth of legend which grew around the figure of Nicholas,[4] Bishop of Myra, to become after his death in 343 one of the great saints of the Eastern Church, was given to the West to share by

---

[3] Karl Young, *The Drama of the Medieval Church* (Oxford, 1933), II, 307.

[4] For excellent summaries of the life and the accumulation and transmission of the legends of St. Nicholas, to supplement the strictly relevant material given here, as also for a fuller treatment of the development of the cult of the saint in Western Europe to be treated later in the chapter, see: Albrecht, pp. 9-16, and Einar Ronsjö: *La Vie de saint Nicolas par Wace* (Lund, 1942), pp. 7-10. For additional bibliography consult Young: *Drama,* II, 487.

Johannes Diaconus of Naples who, in about 880, freely translated into Latin the Greek *Methodius ad Honorem*;⁵ this was a compilation of miracles and biographical details of St. Nicholas, ascribed to Methodius, patriarch of Constantinople from 842 to 846, and was based upon the earliest extant life of the saint, that composed by Michael the Archimandrite between 814 and 842. This first Latin vita of St. Nicholas, a condensation of the work of Methodius with additional material taken from later writers, continued to attract new miracles, among them that of the *Iconia Sancti Nicholai*, originally a Greek legend, the *Thauma de imagine in Africa*,⁶ based on events of the invasion of Calabria by the Saracens at the end of the ninth and in the early tenth centuries. The vita achieved its fullest form in the tenth century in two main redactions, one printed by Mombritius in 1479,⁷ and the other by Falconius in 1751.⁸ The chief difference between these versions lies in the extra material drawn from the life of St. Nicholas of Sion presented in the latter; their respective accounts of the miracles of St. Nicholas of Myra, including that of the *Iconia Sancti Nicholai*, are, with the exception of one miracle which does not concern us here, identical.⁹ Since the vita of Johannes Diaconus is clearly recognizable as the basis of all subsequent versions of the legends in Western Europe, it is to his account of the *Iconia* legend that the account of the same legend in Bodel's miracle play must first be compared.

The legend of the *Iconia Sancti Nicolai* as it appears in the vita of Johannes Diaconus is as follows:[10] An army of Vandals from

---

[5] Text in G. Anrich, *Hagios Nikolaos, der heilige Nikolaos in der griechischen Kirche* (Leipzig, 1913-17), I, 140-150.

[6] Text in Anrich, I, 339 ff.

[7] Boninus Mombritius, ed.: *Sanctuarium seu Vitae Sanctorum* (Milan, 1479), II, 161-170; reprinted: *Sanctuarium seu Vitae Sanctorum, novam hanc Editionem curaverunt duo Monachi solesmenses* (Paris, 1910), II, 296-309.

[8] N. C. Falconius, ed.: *Sancti Confessoris Pontificis et celeberrimi Thaumaturgi Nicolai Acta Primigenia* (Naples, 1751), pp. 112-126. For further information on this edition, see Ronsjö, p. 8, note 7.

[9] For a comparison of Falconius' and Mombritius' editions of the *vita* of Johannes Diaconus, see Ronsjö, pp. 28-38.

[10] Mombritius, II, 306-307. Reprinted with changes in the punctuation by Young, *Drama*, II, 491-492. Quotations in this study are to this more readily accessible reprinting.

Africa sacked Calabria. One of the Vandals (a *barbarus*) found an image in the house of a Christian. Taking it, he learned from a Christian captive that it was an image of St. Nicholas, a great miracle worker. Keeping this information to himself, the *barbarus* returned to Africa with the army. A tax collector (thelonarius) by profession, he was one day called away by his business and, commanding Nicholas to guard his treasure, he left his treasure house open with the image before it and under no other guard. Thieves passing by planned to rob the treasure house that night, which they accordingly did, leaving behind only the image. When the *barbarus* returned he beat the image, beside himself with rage and grief, and threatened to burn it if the treasure were not returned. Stirred by the mistreatment of his image as though he himself had been beaten, St. Nicholas appeared to the robbers as they were dividing the spoil and threatened them with public exposure and death unless they returned the stolen property forthwith. The terrified robbers replaced everything in the treasure house, which caused the *barbarus* this time to weep for joy and, kissing the image, he loudly proclaimed his belief in St. Nicholas and in Christ. He and his household were baptized in the Christian faith and, having built a church to St. Nicholas, he, with his wife and children, spent his time there glorifying God and St. Nicholas.

The second vita of St. Nicholas known to have been in existence in Bodel's day was that of Wace.[11] Composed in about 1150 [12] it was a condensed but close translation into French of the Latin vita of Diaconus. Wace himself tells us:

> En romanz voil dire un petit
> De ceo que nus le latin dit. . . .   (vss. 41-42)
>
> Ci falt le livre mestre Guace
> Qu'il ad de seint Nicholas feit
> De latin en romanz estreit. . . .   (vss. 1546-1548)

Wace's version of the Iconia legend (vss. 651-722) deviates little from the Latin original. After the death of St. Nicholas (the poet

---

[11] Editions: Monmerqué, *Mélanges*, pp. 300-360; N. Delius, *Maistre Wace's St. Nicholas, ein altfranzösisches Gedicht des zwölften Jahrhunderts aus Oxforder Handschriften* (Bonn, 1850); Mary S. Crawford, *Life of St. Nicholas*, University of Pennsylvania dissertation (Philadelphia, 1924); Ronsjö, to which edition all textual references in this study are made.

[12] For the determination of this date, see Ronsjö, pp. 18-26.

relates) there was great grief throughout the land and many people made images which they venerated in his name. It came about that pagans sailed from beyond the seas to plunder the Christians, wreaking great destruction and taking many prisoners. One of the pagans found a beautiful image which he took to a Christian captive for identification. Told that it was of St. Nicholas, a powerful saint who would keep his devotee from poverty, the pagan, still a tax official (tolnoiers), made the image the guardian of his wealth. One day, in his absence, thieves, seeing the treasure without guard, stole everything. The *tolnoiers* angrily beat the image when he returned to find his loss. To save his image, St. Nicholas went to the thieves and ordered them to restore the treasure on pain of exposure and cruel torture. The thieves obeyed and the pagan, out of pleasure, embraced Christianity. Many others also were converted and the country became Christian.

Considering the legend of the image of St. Nicholas as Bodel relates it in the Prologue of his *Jeu*, together with the few details necessary to complete the basic story which are omitted from the Prologue but which can be extracted from the play itself, it appears that, although the versions of Bodel, Johannes and Wace have in common the central theme of a barbarian entrusting his treasure to an image of the saint, losing it to thieves and, upon regaining it through the intercession of the saint, embracing Christianity, it is at once apparent that Bodel is not as dependent upon either of these two earlier versions as Wace is upon Johannes. Neither can it be held that Wace's version is nearer to Bodel's than is the Latin vita, for, despite the probability that Wace's vernacular *vie* was well known and highly thought of in Arras, even fifty years after its composition, it lacks certain details shared by the other accounts. A radical change is immediately evident in Bodel's account of the legend: the reversal of the rôles of Christian and Pagan in the armed invasion which sets the scene for the enactment of the miracle. The Christians invade the land of a neighboring king, " uns rois paiiens/ Qui marchissoit as crestïens " (vss. 9-10), identified as the " roy d'Aufrike," his subjects being generally referred to as pagans but sometimes as Saracens. Diaconus speaks of the Christians being invaded by sea by pagans from Africa: " Cum de Affricae partibus Vandalorum exercitus applicuisset ad terram Calabrindem " (II, 1-2). The Vandals are once referred to as Saracens (l. 40). Wace also tells of a sea-borne invasion of Christians by pagans: " Une feiz vindrent d'ultre mer/ Païens pur cristïens rober " (vss. 659-660), using no other term than *païens* for the pagans and never giving their country of origin. Explicitly stated in the Latin vita is the return of the pagan to his country with the image. Although Wace does not mention this, the reference to the conversion of the pagan country to Christianity shows that here, too, the miracle took place in the homeland of the invaders.

Hand in hand with the transformation of a Saracen raid into a Christian crusade go striking developments and changes in the rôles of the characters of the earlier versions of the legend. The barbarian, a *thelonarius* in Diaconus and a *tolnoeirs* in Wace, becomes the all-powerful king of the Saracens: the ill-defined member of an army, whose only act of significance in the invasion was the seizing of the image as personal plunder, becomes the commander-in-chief of the armies which destroy the invaders and whose vassals hasten from the four corners of the world to his defense and dutifully bring plunder to him. With the image is brought before him the Christian captive, now no longer a figure introduced into the story merely to describe the powers of the image and then to disappear completely, but a living character, essential to the whole subsequent development of the plot. Around him and the King revolves the complex action of the miracle.

These new features in the legend, interdependent and logical developments of the initial reversal of the rôles of invader and invaded, find a natural focus in the miracle exemplifying the powers of St. Nicholas. The claims made by the Christian captive with respect to these powers vary in the three versions, those of the Preudom of Bodel exhibiting a distinctly novel aspect. Diaconus' Christian declares:

Imago haec quam cernimus Sancti Nicolai dicitur, qui multis miraculis et virtutibus apud Deum et homines existens clarus manifeste edocet se uiuere etiam post sepulchrum (ll. 9-11).

The captive of Wace is more specific:

' Forme est,' dist il, ' seint Nicolas.
Ja tant cum tu l'onureras
Ne serras povres ne cheitifs.
Un seint est mult poësteïz.'   (vss. 669-672)

The Preudom is even clearer in his claim and introduces a new element:

> ' Sire, ains est fais en le sanlanche
> Saint Nicolai que je mout aim.
> Pour che l'aour je et reclaim
> Que nus hom qui l'apiaut de cuer
> N'iert ja esgarés a nul fuer;
> Et s'est si bonne garde eslite
> Que il monteploie et pourfite
> Canque on li commande a garder.'   (vss. 32-39)

From the general statement that St. Nicholas is a great miracle worker and the more specific claim that he who venerates the saint will never know poverty, we pass to the most precise declaration: the saint is such an effective guard that he actually increases what is entrusted to him. In addition, however, is the claim—which, it is to be noted, takes pride of place—that he who wholeheartedly appeals to St. Nicholas will never be abandoned. This new miracle or new aspect of the miracle is duly accomplished according to the claim, for when the treasure is stolen and the captive's life is forfeit, he finds himself in a desperate plight, apparently helplessly abandoned to a horrible and imminent death, but, calling upon St. Nicholas to help him, he is saved by the same act which restores the King to prosperity. But although the Preudom is saved by the same act which recovers the treasure, this aspect of the miracle is not to be considered as only an embellishment or even as of minor importance. In its natural and intimate connection with the traditional miracle of the guarding of treasure it is a highly successful graft, strengthening and revitalizing the old stock. It is indispensable in justifying and drawing together the distinctive features of the exposition of the initial events which give to this version of the legend its dramatic qualities and realistic character. These distinctive features create ideal circumstances for the accomplishment of the miracle in its new aspect. A Christian is exposed to the tyranny of a Saracen, the Saracen is a mighty king and so capable of the most absolute tyranny, the Christian is a lone prisoner and therefore completely helpless; finally these circumstances are the natural outcome of an unsuccessful crusade.

The introduction of the new miracle and the conflict of the King with the Preudom involved in it, bring about another significant departure from the predecessors of Bodel. The most vivid feature of their versions of the legend is the mistreatment of the image set to guard the treasure. In each case the outraged pagan beats the image and orders it to return the stolen property immediately; in the account of the Latin vita, moreover, under pain of being burned on the morrow. In the *Jeu*, it is the Preudom who bears the brunt of the pagan's wrath. He is soundly cursed and condemned to death. To allow the robbers time to replace the treasure before the pagan can carry out his dire threats, the pagan has to be restrained for a certain period of time. Bodel alone is able to solve this problem plausibly and he accomplishes it by the most apposite setting in motion of the action of the second miracle. When condemned to death, the Preudom pleads successfully for delay:

>     Le roys commande c'on le fache
>     Morir de mort laide et despite.
>     ' A! roys, pour Dieu! car me respite
>     Anuit mais,' fait li crestïens,
>     ' Savoir se ja de ches lïens
>     Me geteroit sains Nicolais.'   (vss. 72-77)

Here is evidence of the importance of the theme of the saving of a supplicant. No direct mention is made of the recovery of the treasure either here in the Prologue or at the corresponding point in the play. It is in this nicely contrived delay that St. Nicholas appears to the robbers and orders them to give back their booty.

Further differences between the three versions of the legend can be cited to indicate the development of new features in Bodel's *Jeu*, which are particularly at variance with the *vie* of Wace. The *tolnoeirs* appoints the image as guardian of his wealth from the time of learning of the powers of the saint, whereas both the *thelonarius* and the King of Africa test the image for the first time on the crucial occasion. Wace simply narrates the events of the robbery without reference to time. Diaconus lends the same events dramatic impulse by setting the thieves' discovery of the unguarded treasure in the daytime and the theft and replacement of the stolen property with all the intervening events, at night. Bodel expands the incidents over a more clearly defined length of time; his robbers hear of their opportunity for easy wealth by day, and steal and replace the treasure on successive nights, the King awakening the following mornings to find his wealth now stolen, now returned. No mention is made by Wace of how the robbers discovered the absence of the *tolnoeirs* and his exposed riches; Diaconus says that passing by the pagan's house they saw their opportunity and planned their theft for that night. Bodel has one of the thieves hear the King's proclamation announcing that the royal treasure lay open to anyone who cared to take it, a detail of the action made possible by virtue of the pagan now being a King and which is important in the development of the tavern scenes in the play.

The solution of the crisis in each of the three versions follows the same pattern with little variation, all agreeing as to the joy of the pagan at the ultimate success of his risk and as to his immediate conversion to Christianity, with his family (Diaconus), his country (Wace), and the other pagans (Bodel).

Despite the underlying identity of the basic themes in the versions we have examined, the distinctive aspects of Bodel's account— the simple but radical change in the opening situation, characters so changed as scarcely to resemble their earlier counterparts, events following a course new in significant detail and the recasting of the miracle in a new and double form which endows the whole story with a strong inner cohesion—all compel the conclusion that neither in the *vita* of Johannes Diaconus nor in the *vie* of Wace is to be found the precise source of the *Jeu de saint Nicolas*. In expressing this view, disagreement must be sought with Rohnstroem who, despite an assertion of the impossibility of finding the precise source of the *Jeu*, declares it is probably in the *vie* of Wace, basing his theory upon what he sees as the similarity of the two versions and upon the undoubted high literary reputation of Wace in Arras in Bodel's day.[13]

Support for the independence of Bodel's account of the *Iconia legend* may be found in the very references quoted earlier which purport to indicate a written authoritative source. The first of these:

>  Che nous content li voir disant
>  Qu'en sa vie trouvons lisant . . .

may be taken as applying only, or primarily, to the complement of the sentence:

>  Que jadis fu uns rois paiiens
>  Qui marchissoit as crestïens.

---

[13] Rohnstroem, pp. 54-55.

This statement does not tally with the corresponding statements of the earlier versions, both Diaconus and Johannes declaring that the pagans came from overseas. If, on the other hand, the reference is taken to embrace the whole account to follow, then in view of the total discrepancies we have noted, it still argues against a link between Bodel and his predecessors. When the *preecieres* reaches the point in the narrative where the thieves have committed the robbery and have gone to sleep, he decides to abbreviate the legend and pass straight to the King's discovery of the theft:

>Une nuit il troi s'assanlerent,
>Au tresor vinrent, si l'emblerent;
>Et quant il l'en orent porté,
>Si leur donna Diex volenté
>De dormir: tes sommes lor vint
>Qu'iloec endormir les couvint,
>Ne sait ou, en un abitacle.
>Mais pour abregier le miracle,
>M'en passe outre, selonc l'escrit.
>Et quant che sot li rois et vit
>Que son tresor a desmané . . .   (vss. 53-63)

The same phase of the story is treated by Diaconus and Wace as follows:

Nam uenientes [fures] nocte omnia abstulerunt, aurum, argentum, vestes, et caetera, et sic profecti sunt. Sola anchona deforis pendens superstes remansit. Haec autem Dei dispensatione agebantur ut huiuscemodi occasione reperiretur quanti meriti Nicolaus esset, et apud Africanas regiones manifeste clares(c)eret. Veniente autem barbaro, cuius theloneum erat, reperit enim uacuum. . . .   (Diaconus, lines 25-29)

>Sanz garde unt cel aver trové.
>Ne remist ren, tut l'ont emblé.
>Quant li tolonoiers repeirat,
>De son aver ren ne trouvat.   (Wace, vss. 683-686)

The reference to the " escrit " of Bodel at this juncture would seem to be of help in two ways of identifying a source. The implications of his statement are that the original miracle story is here abridged and that the events related are as recorded in that same written work. A comparison of the three versions again shows a discrepancy. Bodel has in no way abbreviated either of the other versions; on the contrary his emphasis on the deep sleep sent by God which overcame the thieves is his peculiarity; in other words, if he were following either Diaconus or Wace, he would not be abridging but expanding his source. As for the second implication, the events following the "abridgement"—the dragging of the Preudom before the King, the sentence of death passed upon him and his successful appeal for one night's respite—although following the same pattern of events, are not the same events as those of the earlier versions. The same circumstances attend the third reference to a source. The King listens to the plea of the Preudom to delay his execution.

> A grant paine l'en fist relais.
> Mais issi le conte le lettre
> Qu'en se chartre le first remettre.  (vss. 78-80)

Again the reference cannot be to Diaconus or to Wace since the incident depends entirely upon the new rôles given to the captive and the pagan in the *Jeu de saint Nicolas*. The fourth and final reference to a written authority appears at the conclusion of the narration of the legend. The whole story is gathered up:

> Signeur, che trouvons en le vie
> Del saint dont anuit est la veille.  (vss. 104-105)

This last claim reinforces the preceding claims, pleading an authoritative source for the whole story, but its very generality offers no contradiction to the evidence of the earlier references and can serve only as a final argument for the contention that neither in Diaconus nor in Wace can we seek a specific source for the *Jeu*.

The source of the *Jeu de saint Nicolas* has also been sought in the two dramatic works treating the same legend, first mentioned by Petit de Julleville, Hilarius' *Ludus Super Iconia Sancti Nicolai*,[14] composed during the first half of the twelfth century and one of the four Nicholas plays in the collection of ten liturgical dramas in the so-called Fleury manuscript, dating from the early twelfth century.[15] Hilarius tells of a certain pagan (*Barbarus*) who con-

[14] Editions: J. J. Champollion-Figeac; E. Du Méril, *Les origines latines du théâtre moderne* (Paris, 1849), and facsimile reproduction (Leipzig and Paris, 1897), pp. 272-276; J. B. Fuller, *Hilarii Versus et Ludi, edited from the Paris manuscript* (New York, 1929), pp. 87-93; J. Q. Adams, *Chief Pre-Shakespearean Dramas* (Boston and New York, 1924), pp. 55-58; A. W. Pollard, *English Miracle Plays, Moralities and Interludes* (Oxford, 1923), pp. 162-165; Young, *Drama*, II, 338-341.

[15] Editions: Monmerqué, *Mélanges*, pp. 111-118; T. Wright, *Early Mysteries and other Latin poems of the twelfth and thirteenth centuries* (Lon-

fidently entrusted his treasure (gold and clothing) to an image of St. Nicholas when he had to go on a journey. Four or six robbers, finding the door open and no guards in sight, stole everything. Upon his return, the *Barbarus*, in grief and rage, violently abused the image, beat it and threatened further beating if the stolen property were not returned. St. Nicholas appeared to the robbers, blamed them for the beating he had received and ordered them to return what they had stolen, under threats of exposure and punishment. The thieves did as they were ordered and the *Barbarus*, in wondrous delight, begged forgiveness of the image. The saint appeared to the *Barbarus*, telling him to thank God, not him. The pagan accordingly renounced his past errors and declared his belief in God and Christ. The Fleury play concerns a Jew [16] who was in the habit of venerating an image of St. Nicholas which he kept hidden in his house. When he had become rich, business one day compelled his absence and he left his treasure (gold, silver, and clothing) in an unlocked chest with the image as sole guardian. Three robbers passed by and, deciding to take the opportunity to rob the Jew, discovered the chest. Finding it too heavy to lift, however, they opened it and made off with its contents. The Jew returned and, lamenting his loss, reviled the untrustworthy Nicholas and promised to beat the image the next day as he was too tired to do so that night. The saint appeared to the thieves, blamed them for the harsh treatment his image had received and ordered them to return their loot that night under pain of public exposure and torture. The thieves did his bidding but only after a discussion as to whether to give up their new found wealth or not. The Jew, overjoyed at the restoration of his goods, called

don, 1838), pp. 11-14; Du Méril, *Origines*, pp. 266-271; E. de Coussemaker, *Drames liturgiques du moyen âge* (Rennes, 1860), pp. 109-122; Young, *Drama*, II, 344-348; Albrecht, pp. 129-134. References in this study are to this last named edition.

[16] Albrecht, pp. 43-44, suggests that the transformation of the Saracen into a Jew is a touch of local color, Jews being particularly numerous in the Orléanais in the Middle Ages. This, however, is a change of detail which in no way affects the course of the events nor the characterization in the story, and to use it as a means of establishing a distinct category of the versions of the legend, as does Rohnstroem (p. 54) and Warne (p. xiv), is to falsify the whole picture of the interrelationships of the many versions of the legend.

upon those present to praise St. Nicholas and to turn from their idols to the Christian saint.

It may easily be seen how these plays lend support to the supposition that the *vita* of Johannes Diaconus, as it appears in the edition of Mombritius, was widely current in the twelfth century, for not only does the theme of each correspond closely to the central part of the Diaconus account but each, as the differences between them show, is unquestionably directly inspired by it. Of greater interest here, however, is their possible relationship to Bodel's version, suggested by features they share exclusively with the story of the French miracle play. Passing from the Latin *vita*, we notice a fresh feature in Hilarius' *ludus*, the reappearance of the saint to the *Barbarus* to direct his thanks to God, the effect which is to make the conversion of the pagan to Christianity more plausible. A similar effect is obtained in the *Jeu* of Bodel. The Saracen King, in view of his character, might reasonably be expected merely to welcome the image of St. Nicholas as another, more powerful idol, and although Bodel guards against this by revealing the conversion in the Prologue and by such devices within the play as the assurance of the Angel to the Preudom that

> Le roi convertiras
> Et ses barons metras
> Fors de leur fole loy;
> Et si tenront le foy
> Que tienent crestien [che croy.]   (vss. 555-559)

The Preudom reinforces the plausibility of the conversion of the King when called before him after the restoration of the treasure (Sc. XXXIII) by attempting to correct the monarch's wild enthusiasm for the saint alone by both his own prayer of thanks to God and his invitation to the King to surrender to God as well as to St. Nicholas:

> Diex, aourés en soies tu
> Que de te grasce as ravestu
> Cest roy qui encontre toi ert!
> Sire, faus est qui te mescroit
> Et qui de toi servir recroit,
> Car te vertus reluist et pert.
> Rois, giete te folie puer,
> Si te ren de mains et de cuer
> A Dieu, qu'il ait de toi pitié,
> Et au baron saint Nicolai.   (vss. 1449-1458)

That this similarity between Hilarius' *Ludus* and Bodel's *Jeu* is attributable to direct influence is open to question, all the more so since these two plays share no other exclusive feature. The *Iconia* play of Fleury, on the other hand, although it, too, has only one feature exclusively in common with the *Jeu de saint Nicolas*, might therein have influenced it strongly. That feature is the expansion of the phase of the narrative centering around the actions of the thieves, a similarity in gross and in detail. In the first of the two scenes which may be compared we learn that there are three robbers and that the treasure is in a chest which they find too heavy to remove bodily:

PRIMUS dicat:

>     Arcam istam hinc tollite,
>     si potestis, quam concite;
>     quod si nequitis, frangite;
>     que sunt in ea, capite.

Quo dicto, fingant se non posse leuare arcam; et dicat SECUNDUS:

>     Nos oportet hanc archam frangere,
>     quam nequimus integram tollere.

Tunc ueniens TERCIUS, et inueniens seram non fermam, dicat:

>     O quanta exultacio!
>     hec archa, magno gaudio,
>     se reserari uoluit
>     et se nobis aperuit.

Hoc dicto, capto quod fuerit in archa, abeant.   (*Iconia*, vss. 36-46)

CLIKÉS

>     Rasoir, che bon escrin pesant
>     Prendés, car che sont tout besant . . .

RASOIRS

>     A, vif dïable! Que il poise!
>     Pinchedé, met che sac plus prés:
>     Chis escrins poise comme un grés,
>     Pour un petit qu'il ne me crieve.

PINCEDÉS

>     Rue chaiens tout a un fais,
>     N'ai talent que l'escrin i lais.   (*Jeu*, vss. 1004-1011)

When it comes to returning the treasure, the thieves in each case show unwillingness to lose so easily their booty and give some thought to disobeying the saint. Wise counsel, however, prevails:

Recedente sancto, dicat UNUS ex eis:
>Quanta mors est has gazas reddere!
>si laudatis, uolo diuidere.

ALIUS:
>In isto negocio
>egemus consilio
>nunquam letus fuero
>si hec sic reddidero.

TERCIUS:
>Est melius hec nobis reddere,
>quam sic uitam pendendo perdere.

OMNES insimul:
>Redeamus
>et reddamus.   (*Iconia*, vss. 91-101)

>PINCEDÉS
>Segneur, or creés m'estoutie!
>Prengne chascuns une pugnie
>De ches besans: ja n'i parroit!

>CLIKÉS
>Tais te, faus! Il nous mesquerroit,
>S'en porriemes estres repris!

>RASOIRS
>Met le chi, car chi fu il pris,
>Si remet l'ymage deseure.   (*Jeu*, vss. 1351-1357)

In view of these similarities to aspects of the *Jeu de saint Nicolas*, strong in the case of the Fleury play, if slight in the case of Hilarius' *Ludus*, it is highly probable that Bodel was familiar at least with the former and was directly influenced by it. It is possible that, inspired by the occasion of the feast of St. Nicholas or at the behest of a patron or a *puy*, to write a miracle in honor of the saint, Bodel did not independently choose the *Iconia* legend as his precise subject; the use of this particular legend may have been suggested to him by one of these earlier dramas. It is even possible that his motivation was not principally the celebration of St. Nicholas' Eve but a desire to emulate or improve upon these plays. Insofar as this could be so, it may be claimed that Bodel was inspired by one of these earlier dramas. What has not the same degree of speculation is the assertion that the *Jeu* was not modelled upon nor a reworking of these plays. Neither can be regarded as the precise source. Each is a dramatization of only a section of the story of the legend, excluding all events leading up to the moment of entrusting the treasure to the image, whereas Bodel's versions of the story embraces the complete series of events from the initial conflict between the pagans and the Christians to the ultimate conversion of the barbarian. Moreover, each of these earlier plays, as has been noted, is very close to the narrative of the Diaconus *vita*, and offers no precedent for the particular features which distinguish the *Jeu de saint Nicolas*. The similarities emerging from the above comparison may indicate influence but only in detail, not in Bodel's radical departure from the main threads of narrative of the traditional legend.

The conclusion that Bodel's version of the Iconia legend is essentially independent of the Hilarius *Ludus* and the liturgical play from the Fleury manuscript, just as it was independent of the version of Wace and of Johannes Diaconus, makes unacceptable the theory of Fissen, who regarded it as a free adaptation of the Latin miracle plays, chiefly that of Fleury, with reminiscences of Diaconus and Wace.[17]

There remains for consideration the possibility of Bodel's *Jeu* being based on some lost version of the *Iconia* legend of St. Nicholas. It is argued that in view of the great popularity of this saint in the eleventh and twelfth centuries and of the great number of miracles attributed to him, there must have existed an infinite number of variations of those legends, one of which might well have provided Bodel with the material as he presents it.[18] In the very intensity of the cult of St. Nicholas, however, and in the very multiplicity of permanent expressions of and recorded references to his legends, lies the rebuttal of such a thesis.

It is scarcely within the power of the twentieth century mind to imagine the deep devotion of the medieval man to St. Nicholas and the great and widespread reputation of the saint as a miracle worker, equalling that of the greatest saints. Yet the lesson, when not directly expressed, is implicit wherever the voice of the Middle Ages can be heard. The medieval iconography of French churches, as Emile Mâle has shown,[19] conveys it: "Saint Martin et saint

[17] K. Fissen, *Das Leben des heiligen Nikolaus in der altfranzösischen Literatur und seine Quellen*, Göttingen dissertation (Göttingen, 1921), pp. 72-77.

[18] Rohnstroem, p. 54; Warne, p. xiv.

[19] E. Mâle, *L'Art religieux du XIIIe siècle en France* (Paris, 1925), pp. 327-333.

Nicolas étaient vénérés comme les plus grands faiseurs de miracles qu'il y ait jamais eu. L'un était le thaumaturge de l'Occident, l'autre celui de l'Orient. Au portail méridional de Chartres, ils ont été placés l'un en face de l'autre: l'intention de mettre les deux grands saints en parallèle est visible." [20] From Mâle's study we learn that, in their profusion, the images of St. Nicholas in sculptured stone and stained glass in the cathedrals of France rivaled those of St. Martin and St. James. Preserved are those of Chartres, Auxerre, Le Mans, Rouen, Bourges, Tours, Saint-Julien-du-Sault in Burgundy, and Saint-Rémi at Reims. Linked with these manifestations of the cult of the saint was the popularity of the pilgrimages to his shrine at Bari in Apulia where his relics rested after 1087 when Normans from Southern Italy brought them from Myra in Asia Minor, and later to the shrine in the church of Saint-Nicolas du Port at Varangueville in Lorraine, where certain relics were brought from Bari. These pilgrimages seem to have drawn as many devotees as did those to the shrines of St. James of Compostella and St. Martin of Tours. These different expressions of the cult were undoubtedly directly connected, the pilgrimages stimulating the iconographical representations and vice-versa, but underlying both was a deep desire to celebrate and honor the saint, the protector of sailors, children and merchants, men and women, and indeed of all those oppressed and in danger.

This phenomenal cult [21] was not restricted to France. Even before the translation of his relics to Bari and the beginning of pilgrimages there, St. Nicholas was widely venerated in Europe, in Italy, France, Germany, and England, but it was not until the fame of the miraculous powers of the oil flowing from the tomb of the saint at Bari was spread by pilgrims that the cult began to exceed ordinary proportions and the number of shrines throughout Western Europe to increase towards the magnificent total of more than two thousand.[22]

[20] Mâle, p. 331.

[21] Albrecht (pp. 13-14), and Ronsjö (pp. 9-10), each give useful concise summaries of the general development of the cult. For the fullest treatment, however, which both utilize, see K. Meisen, *Nikolauskult und Nikolausbrauch im Abendlande, eine kultgeographisch-volkskundliche Untersuchung*, in *Forschungen zur Volkskunde*, IX-XII (Duesseldorf, 1931), pp. 71- 93.

[22] Listed by Meisen, pp. 126-171.

In the light of the popularity and widespread devotion to St. Nicholas, the sermon, attributed now to St. Bernard [23] and now to Peter Damian,[24] is more readily understood. The preacher first comments on the profusion of legends round the figure of the saint: " Tot enim et tanta miracula cumulantur, ut omnes litteratorum argutiae vix ad scribendum sufficiant, nos ad legendum." St. Nicholas is to be accorded the highest honor: " Nonne post memoriam Virginis singularis, tam dulcis pietas, vel pia dulcedo in cordibus fidelium observatur ut in die tribulationis nomen Nicolai teneatur in ore, requiescat in corde? " In all times of stress and trouble it is of him that help is at once sought; he is beloved by all: " Juvenes et virgines, senes cum junioribus laudent nomen eius."

The *Iconia* legend, but one of the many legends of this great thaumaturge, was the subject of many manifestations of his cult in the twelfth and thirteenth centuries. Literary expression, in addition to the French *Vie* of Wace and the two Latin plays discussed above, is to be seen in one Latin poem of the twelfth century [25] and in a sermon of Honorius of Autun.[26] References to the legend are frequent in hymns of both this and the following century.[27] In the thirteenth century it is related in the *Legenda Aurea* of Jacobus de Voragine, in an anonymous French prose life [28] and in the *Speculum historiale* of Vincent of Beauvais.[29]

---

[23] *PL*, CLXXXIV, 1055.

[24] *PL*, CXLIV, 835.

[25] T. Wright and J. O. Halliwell, *Reliquiae Antiquae. Scraps from ancient manuscripts, illustrating early English literature and the English language* (London, 1843), I, 202-203. Albrecht also mentions an unpublished Latin poem in a Rouen manuscript.

[26] *PL*, CLXXII, 1030.

[27] Albrecht, p. 45.

[28] MS. 307 (formerly 852) in the Bibliothèque d'Arras, printed in Monmerqué, *Mélanges*, pp. 258-263. Ch. Foulon, in " La représentation et les sources du *Jeu de saint Nicolas*," *Mélanges offerts à Gustave Cohen* (Paris, 1950), pp. 55-66, supposes that this MS, although written at the end of the thirteenth century, dates back to a version of the *Iconia* legend known to Bodel. He sees in it and in the *Vie* of Wace, the principal sources of Bodel's *Jeu*. His comparison of the themes of the various versions of the legend (p. 61)—those of the *Legenda Aurea*, the Fleury play, Hilarius' play, the MS. 307 of Arras, the *Vie* of Wace and Bodel's *Jeu* (no comparison is made to the Diaconus version)—on which he bases his conclusion, although recognizing the reversal of the rôles of the Saracens and the

The same legend is also frequently encountered in the inconography of French churches from the thirteenth century on; at Chartres, Tours, Rouen, Le Mans, Saint-Julien-le-Sault, Troyes, and Auxerre, it was depicted in stained glass in varying degrees of detail.[30] In Germany, in addition to pictorial representation it appeared in written form three times during the thirteenth century. It is also narrated in the North and South English and Scottish Legendaries.[31]

The salient feature of these varied and widely distributed representations of the legend of the *Iconia Sancti Nicolai*, in verse and prose narrative and in dramatic form, in sculpture and stained glass, is their marked uniformity of subject and their conformity to the nuclear *vita* of Johannes Diaconus, leaving the version of Bodel standing in isolation. The close dependence of the written forms of the legend and allusions to it, upon the Latin version are firmly established by textual comparison. Similarly, the pictorial forms, when sufficiently detailed to allow of positive identification, clearly indicate the same source, since they all depict its characteristic feature, the barbarian (or Jew) either entrusting his house to the image or in the act of beating it. In corroboration of this view of the independence of Bodel's account, this characteristic pictorial representation of the legend may be seen in strong contrast to the sole pictorial representation according to Bodel, the miniature preceding the text in the manuscript, which shows, not the pagan beating the image but the Preudom kneeling before the mitred image of St. Nicholas, illustrating the unique character of the play.

The great popularity of St. Nicholas and the multitude of versions of or references to the *Iconia* legend may be considered as an indication, not that among an infinite number of versions there might have existed the model for Bodel's story, but, on the contrary, that it is highly improbable that such a model existed. All

---

Christians in the initial invasion, takes no account of the other distinctive aspects of the *Jeu* treated above, notably the rôles of the King and the Preudom and the new double aspect of the miracle. In view of the date of this MS, of the necessity for considering Diaconus in comparing versions of the legend, and of the unique features of Bodel's *Jeu*, the validity of M. Foulon's findings must be disputed.

[29] Vincent de Beauvais, *Speculum historiale*, 4 vols. (Strasburg, 1473).
[30] Albrecht, pp. 71-73.
[31] Albrecht, pp. 46-47.

the manifestations cited above attest a conservative adherence to the form of the legend as it appears in the *vita* of Johannes Diaconus, the only variations being the characterization of the pagan as a Jew and omissions or condensations of parts of the narrative. None foreshadow the unique features of Bodel's version, the double nature of the miracle, the characterization of the Preudom and the King and the crusading nature of the clash between the Christians and Saracens. No version or reference to a version exists to show a deviation from the traditional legend sufficient to indicate a possible development towards an ultimate version akin to that of Bodel. Had such a version or tendency existed there would assuredly have remained traces of it in some stage of its development away from the traditional legend in some of the many representations we have passed under review. It is not necessary, however, to rely exclusively upon negative evidence, strong though it may be, to disprove the existence of a significant variation of the legend. The *Iconia Sancti Nicolai* is not unique in such a lack; this is characteristic of hagiographical legends in general. The initial impulse in the perpetuation of the memory of a saintly figure, springing from an incident, a place, or some myth connected with him, results in a series of legends describing aspects of his life and death, and miracles wrought by him, both during his life and after. Just as the saint himself tends to lose his individuality in the course of the oral evolution of these legends, becoming an unreal, vague figure endowed with all virtues and powers and scarcely distinguishable from other saints, so do the legends themselves tend quickly to become stereotyped, invariable stories, reduced to simple essential themes, devitalized as it were, and susceptible of no change. The only development possible is the later addition to the series of legendary events, of others prompted by some new connection with the saint, often borrowed from some other *vita*, illustrating new facets of his life or works and tending to identify him even more closely with the generic saint. Thus the portrait becomes a catalogue or program. " Et ce programme est bien peu varié. Car la pauvreté de l'invention est encore une des caractéristiques de l'intelligence de la multitude. Ses développements sont toujours les mêmes et ses combinaisons peu intéressantes. Quant à ses facultés créatrices, elles paraissent vouées à la stérilité dès qu'elle est en possession d'un certain nombre de motifs suffisamment intéressants et de thèmes assez nombreux pour s'adapter à la plupart des situations." [32] The *vita* of Johannes Diaconus followed this general pattern. The miracles comprising the life of St. Nicholas which he translated from Greek were already in this fixed, ultimate form and the only change affected by him and by his successors was the addition of new legends reduced by oral report to the same simple and sterile form which resisted change for two centuries, despite the rapid and extensive development of the cult of which they were a part.

The search for a specific source for the *Jeu de saint Nicolas* leads, then, to the conclusion that none existed. Bodel's version must be regarded as unique. While preserving the same basic theme and utilizing its material, he gave the legend new life by freeing it from the restraint of the traditional form, breaking the mold in which it was cast two hundred years earlier, then adding to it and taking away from it, obeying only the dictates of his poetic imagination and inventive genius, he created an essentially new work.

The establishing of the originality of the basic plot of the *Jeu de saint Nicolas* leaves us with the outstanding question of the meaning and significance of the author's apparent references to a written authority. They are not to be dismissed as a mere poetic convention; [33] the insistence in making such an appeal four times in a little over one hundred lines and the particular circumstances of each instance demand closer attention and a positive explanation.

The prologue in medieval drama is essentially functional. It may be defined as an introductory speech made by the author, a member of the company, or a cleric, to enjoin silence upon the audience, to give them an understanding of the plot, often in the form of a lengthy analysis of the play, as a vehicle for a prayer or sermon, or for the moral lesson exemplified in the play, and for the apologies or other explanations the author may wish to present in order to forestall adverse criticism. It may also contain explanations of the stage setting and the introduction of the characters.[34] The object of Bodel's Prologue is clearly not moral, and any purpose of describing the setting of the action or the characters is indeed secondary. The appeals to the audience to give ear, first

---

[32] H. Delahaye, "Les légendes hagiographiques," *RQH*, Nouvelle Série, XXX (1903), p. 74.

[33] Del Valle de Paz, p. 100.

[34] D. H. Carnahan, *The Prologue in the Old French and Provençal Mystery*, Yale dissertation (New Haven, 1905), p. 1.

to the Prologue and then to the play, are so brief as to appear to be mere convention:

> Oiiés, oiiés, seigneur et dames,
> Que Diex vous soit garans as ames! (vss. 1-2)
>
> Or nous faites pais, si l'orrés. (vs. 114)

Apart from these initial and concluding lines, the Prologue consists entirely of a detailed analysis of the plot and Bodel's insistence upon his fidelity to some written saint's life. As has been noted above, in comparing Bodel's to other versions of the legend, the first three appeals to authority were made to support what transpire as the most original features of the story, the contiguity of the countries of the Saracens and Christians, and the events involving the unique relationship of Preudom and King. The final appeal is broader in scope, a claim that the whole story as told is that found in the life of the saint. Having thus insisted upon the conformity of the story to a model, Bodel is at further pains to convince the audience that what they will see in the play will be perfectly acceptable because it will be a faithful reproduction of what has been outlined in the Prologue.

> Signeur, che trouvons en le vie
> Del saint dont anuit est la veille.
> Pour che n'aiés pas grant merveille
> Se vous vées aucun affaire;
> Car canques vous nous verrés faire
> Sera essamples sans douter
> Del miracle representer
> Ensi con je devisé l'ai. (vss. 104-111)

Whether there is to be seen in these lines an allusion to the highly original development, in the play to follow, of the scenes concerning the robbers and the Saracens or merely the assurance that basic events of the legend as presented in the Prologue will be faithfully followed, may be open to question. What is finally clear is the character of the Prologue itself. Ostensibly calling the audience to order and putting them in a mood of attentive anticipation of the drama, Bodel betrays by his clear exposition of a legend so changed as to be new, and by his heavy emphasis on a non-existent authority, his awareness of departure from tradition and a strong desire to disguise what might otherwise be taken for undue liberties with the "official" *vita* of the Church. Playwrights living long after Bodel were at great pains not to offend authority, as apologies in their prologues show,[35] for fear of incurring the displeasure not only of the clerics, official guardians of authority, but also of the unofficial but more immediately demonstrative guardian, the common man, as jealous of the integrity of established authority as were those who wielded it over him.

Our attention has so far been confined chiefly to the Prologue of the *Jeu de saint Nicolas*, which we have seen as a careful account of a revitalized legend of St. Nicholas, the originality of which Bodel has deliberately concealed in order to allay the criticisms of a conservative audience. Yet with the opening scenes of the play itself the pretense of adhering to a conventional legend seems to be boldly cast aside and the action and tone of the drama would seem to bear but little resemblance to a dramatization of a *vita*. Indeed, the consensus of critics, as we have seen in the introductory chapter, has been that Bodel was not interested primarily, if at all, in dramatizing the *Iconia* legend; he made of it only an excuse for presenting stirring crusading action and amusing tavern scenes, the latter being of greatest interest (we are told) both to him and his audience.[36] It is only possible to subscribe to this view, however, by ignoring the lesson of the Prologue and by dismissing it as an empty formality. Neither course would seem to be justifiable. The Prologue is such a deliberate composition that to recognize in it no significance would be to make of Bodel a most inconsistent author. Why would he elaborate a carefully constructed prologue and go to such lengths to make his plot acceptable if it were to be but a pretext for a *comédie de mœurs*, relieved by a spectacular crusading scene? We must accept the Prologue as a true introduction to the play and discover in it an implicit poetic aim to be fulfilled in the play depending upon it.

The inability of critics to reconcile the Prologue with the drama proper stems from a misunderstanding of Bodel's intention. This was not merely to reproduce on the stage the events narrated in the traditional legend of St. Nicholas. In freeing the old legend from its conventional restraints and in creating an original version to illustrate the old theme, he was prompted, it is submitted, by more than a desire to give free rein to his inventive faculties. Inspired by the season of the feast of the saint, and perhaps in emula-

---

[35] Carnahan, pp. 75 and 77.
[36] Gaston Paris, *Littérature*, p. 240.

tion of seasonal plays he had seen, his primary object was to celebrate and glorify the saint in a manner befitting the place and occasion. This could most effectively be done by choosing a particular legend and, while preserving the spiritual integrity of the theme, recreating it to fit the local, contemporary scene, or, to express it more simply, to bring it up to date. With a poet's intuition of the place of St. Nicholas in the daily life of his contemporary world, Bodel conceived his *Jeu*. He sought to express the attitude of his fellow citizens of Arras to the saint who heard their prayers in times of distress and to illustrate for their benefit his virtues and powers in familiar terms. In this Bodel is true to the general medieval pattern of representing the divine, the historic and the exotic in human, contemporary, and local terms and colors. His particular success in following this pattern, however, springs from his deliberate adoption of a precise human, contemporary and local point of view, not because he knew no other, but because it was the conception of the saint from this precise point of view that inspired his drama. The sincerity of the devotion of the common man of the twelfth and thirteenth centuries to St. Nicholas is beyond doubt when we stop to consider the extraordinary manifestation of his cult. Bodel sensed the disparity between this living spirit of devotion and the moribund nature of the traditional *vita* which was, nevertheless, a part of it. The traditional legend, even in the form of liturgical or school drama, was an austere, distant story, belonging to the Church and to those who understood Latin and, even in the translation of Wace, it had the cold tones of the tenth century biographer speaking to another audience of another St. Nicholas. Bodel wanted to speak as a living man to his fellows, of the St. Nicholas they knew.

Bodel was fully aware of the revolutionary nature of his drama, but, at the same time he could be confident of faithfully adhering to the spirit of the legend he proposed to treat, and of himself serving St. Nicholas more effectively than if he were mechanically to transpose the outmoded *vita* into dramatic form. He was, in a real sense, justified in decrying his own originality, for his conception of the legend was based on the most authoritative source, what was in his discriminating eye the substantial truth.[37] He could not

[37] In effect Bodel was exhibiting another facet of medieval artistic representation: the "gloss." As L. Spitzer shows in "The Prologue to the *Lais* of Marie de France and Medieval Poetics," *MP*, XLI (1943), 97, note

have doubted the welcoming approval his miracle play would receive from his audience. They would recognize familiar characters, actions, and settings of their own world of Arras as well as those of the often portrayed world of Christian and Saracen conflict firmly fixed in their imaginations, and, above all, they would recognize in St. Nicholas the saint they were familiar with in their every-day existence. In order to assure the play of that welcome, however, it was necessary to overcome the initial obstacle of the audiences's innate conservatism. They had to be given the essential story of the play, fully and clearly, and any objections that might arise therefrom had to be met at the outset in order to allay, at once, suspicions of deviating from tradition and truth. This was accomplished by the references to an authoritative-sounding source. At the conclusion of the Prologue, then, the audience would be satisfied as to the interest and authenticity of the drama to follow. A mood of acceptance would be created which might continue unbroken throughout the course of the play or at least long enough for the action to have captured the interest of the audience sufficiently to override any belated objections they might have on the grounds of a lack of accord with the traditional presentation of a legend. To the more discerning among them, however, any such qualms would be stilled not merely by the presentation of an entertaining miracle play but by the realization that it did excellently convey the true lesson of the legend of the *Iconia Sancti Nicolai*.

In successive chapters an attempt will be made to show how Bodel achieved the expression of his intuition of the St. Nicholas of his time and place, by examining in turn the African and the Arras elements and the manner in which these apparently disparate features are developed and fused in the service of the *Iconia* legend of St. Nicholas, presenting through the medium of the drama a consistent and balanced view of one aspect of the medieval scene.

2, " If we consider a gloss as being based upon an original text, then, in such a case, this " text " must be the life actually lived by the hero: the hero becoming thereby a 'source' of manifold legends (glosses). From every hero, as from every saint, there emanates a legendary tradition, a 'glose' superadded to the original text of his life. Every exemplary life is a Bible—and who says Bible says exegesis." Applying this to the *Jeu* we may consider Bodel as " glossing " an incident in the life of St. Nicholas, which life in itself is the text, the *vie*, the *escrit*, the *lettre*, referred to in the Prologue.

## CHAPTER III

### Epic and Crusade

The crusading aspect of the Christian-Saracen conflict which provides the setting for the miracle of the *Iconia* legend of St. Nicholas, already apparent in the Prologue, is fully developed in the play itself, to the extent that the scenes directly involving Christians and Saracens present in themselves a miniature *chanson de geste*. This may be summarized as follows: the Saracen King of Africa is informed by his messenger, Auberon, that a Christian army has invaded his territory. Infuriated, the King curses the statue of his god, Tervagant, but on the advice of the Seneschal begs the idol's forgiveness and seeks his help and assurance as to the outcome of this emergency. Scarcely encouraged by the idol's prophecy of immediate victory but ultimate defeat, the King issues a general call to arms to repel the invaders. The royal order is proclaimed and Auberon speeds to the four corners of the Saracen empire to summon the assistance of the Emirs of Coine, Orkenie, Oliferne, and Outre le Sec Arbre. These vassals hasten to answer the call of their overlord and rush to his defense with men and treasure. When the Christians see the enemy advancing upon them in overwhelming numbers they resign themselves to death, determined to sell their lives dearly, encouraged by an angel of God who appears to them to exhort them to fight well and with the promise of a place in Paradise. Battle is joined and, as says the rubric, " Or tuent li Sarrasin tous les Crestïens." Here follow the events reported in some detail in the Prologue, the capture of the Preudom and the testing of the powers of St. Nicholas, culminating in the doubling of the King's treasure and conversion to Christianity of the King and his vassals. This conversion, however, is not accomplished without the need of physical force to make Orkenie renounce his faith, which provides the main action of the final scene, suitably brought to a close by the humiliation and destruction of the idol Tervagant.

Since Le Roy, critics in turn have praised the crusading features of the *Jeu*, although, as we have seen, not agreeing upon their importance to the overall understanding of the play. Their attention, however, has been focused mainly upon the single episode of the battle scene, outstanding as a lofty and moving expression of the courage and faith of the Christian warrior. This scene has been universally recognized as inspired by the crusading spirit which animated Europe in the twelfth century, but it has not been fully recognized as also a product of the characteristic literary expression of that spirit, the *chanson de geste*. Little attention has been paid to the particular series of events outlined above in which, when the crusading aspect of the *Jeu* is under consideration, the battle scene must take its place, although its lyrical beauty and Christian character lend it a certain autonomy and set it in sharp relief against the less inspired and often grotesque preceding and following scenes predominantly Saracen in cast. Thus, despite comparisons made to the *Chanson de Roland* in particular and to the heroic literature of France in general, the relationship and indebtedness of the *Jeu de saint Nicolas* to the *chansons de geste* remains for investigation. Since the *Jeu* was written at the end of the great century of the epic, since Bodel himself was a jongleur and the composer of a *chanson de geste*—the *Chanson de Saisnes*—and since the play contains a *chanson de geste* in miniature, clearly recognizable as such to the contemporary audience from the opening lines, such an investigation would seem to be profitable.

The critic to show most awareness of the incomplete nature of the criticism of the crusading element in the *Jeu de saint Nicolas* was Alfred Jeanroy.[1] Noting that the epic grandeur of certain scenes of the play have often been admired and by no means disputing the belief that Bodel wrote them under the influence of sincere crusading emotions, he remarks: " Il n'est que juste toutefois de signaler que ce sont les chansons de geste qui lui ont fourni les couleurs dont il s'est servi et un certain nombre de détails dont il a orné ses tableaux." Nevertheless, apart from the reminder that the name Auberon was taken from *Huon de Bordeaux*, the article is devoted to reminiscences in the *Jeu* of only one *chanson de geste, Fierabras*.[2] In three places in Bodel's play does Jeanroy find simi-

[1] Alfred Jeanroy, " Réminiscences de *Fierabras* dans le *Jeu de saint Nicolas* de Jean Bodel," *Rom.*, L (1924), 435-438.

[2] *Fierabras, chanson de geste, publiée pour la première fois d'après les manuscrits de Paris, de Rome et de Londres*, eds. A. Kroeber and G. Servois, *APF* (Paris, 1860).

larities with this epic, amounting, in his opinion, to more than "une recontre fortuite." Two of the three points of comparison are doubly interesting for, since they involve passages from Saracen episodes, we are encouraged in attempting to place the familiar battle scene in its true context; that is, in the series of events both Christian and Saracen which make up a story of the epic type. If we continue along the way indicated by Jeanroy, it is possible greatly to extend his findings. In every phase of the crusading story embedded in the *Jeu* may be detected reminiscences of, if not direct borrowings from, not only *Fierabras* but many other *chansons de geste*. The story is, in fact, virtually the sum of mostly commonplace elements taken from the epics, exhibiting, moreover, the same alternating focus of attention upon the Christian and Saracen groups of personages whose conflict is the mainspring of the action in French epic literature.[3]

In the *Jeu* the Christian element of the crusading story is concentrated in the single episode of the battle between the forces of the King of Africa and the invading Christians. Within this episode, however, the beauty of the words of the *Crestïens nouviaus chevaliers* has monopolized critical attention at the expense of the scenes' other and broader aspects. Seen against the background of the *chanson de geste* tradition, however, the several discernible aspects of this Christian episode become significant for their particular contribution to the richness and unity of Bodel's *Jeu*.

[3] "La grande idée qui a présidé à la formation de notre épopée, qui lui a donné son caractère essentiel et a été le point de départ de son développement, peut se définir ainsi: la lutte de l'Europe chrétienne contre les Sarrasins sous l'hégémonie de la France." Gaston Paris, *Histoire poétique de Charlemagne* (Paris, 1905), pp. 15-16.

For a review of the historical basis of this conflict between the French and the Saracens, see W. W. Comfort, "The character types in the Old French *chansons de geste*," *PMLA*, XXI (1906), 405-407.

The identity of the "Saracens" of Old French literature is succinctly described by Anouar Hatem, *Les poèmes épiques des Croisades*, thèse pour le doctorat d'université (Paris, 1932), p. 31: "C'est ce duel séculaire entre Charlemagne et Mahomet qui constitue la seule unité de l'épopée française au Moyen Age. Les Normands, Les Huns, les Saxons, les Slaves, tous les Barbares, tous les Païens, les Francs eux-mêmes avant leur conversion se transforment en ' Sarrasins.' "

See also, W. W. Comfort, "The literary rôle of the Saracens in the French epic," *PMLA*, LV (1940), 628-659.

The essential situation in the battle episode is that of a Christian army, faced by overwhelming numbers of Saracens, deliberately and courageously accepting battle and annihilation. Warne suggests that it was this situation, together with the rough treatment of the Preudom, which necessitated the Prologue and its assurance of a successful outcome, because medieval audiences were very impressionable and the representation of such events without some preliminary explanation " might well have led to ugly scenes during the performance." [4] Impressionable as the medieval audience undoubtedly were, it is scarcely thinkable that they would find this situation unacceptable. They would be deeply stirred but sympathetically so, as they were by the telling of countless *chansons de geste* whose appeal lay precisely in the ebb and flow of Christian fortunes through the course of countless battles with the Saracens, in which the odds were almost invariably hugely in favor of the heathen and in which the seriousness of the Christian losses was always emphasized. In particular would the situation created by Bodel recall probably the two oldest, greatest, and most familiar epics, the *Chanson de Roland*,[5] recounting the magnificent defeat at Roncevaux, and the *Chanson de Guillaume*,[6] in which equal prominence is given to the total destruction of a Christian army at l'Archamp where, in a double disaster, first Vivien's troops and then the rescuing forces of William are slaughtered by the Saracens of Desramé. The latter disaster is also the subject of *Aliscans*, differing in detail from the account in the *Chanson de Guillaume* but again describing in ruthless fashion the annihilation of a Christian army.

The reaction of the Christians of Bodel's play to the appearance of the advancing enemy calls to mind that of Oliver when the Saracen trap is sprung at Roncevaux. From Bodel's African battlefield goes up the cry:

> Sains Sepulcres, aïe! Segneur, or du bien faire!
> Sarrasin et paien vienent pour nous fourfaire:
> Vés les armes reluire: tous li cuers m'en esclaire.

---

[4] Warne, p. xvii.

[5] *La chanson de Roland   Publiée d'après le manuscrit d'Oxford et traduite*, ed. Joseph Bédier (Paris, 1922), vol. 1.

[6] *La chanson de Guillaume*, ed. Duncan McMillan, *SATF*, 2 vols. (Paris, 1949).

> Or le faisons si bien que no proueche i paire;
> Contre chascun des nos sont bien, par devise.  (vss. 396-400)

These words are, in effect, a condensation of a passage in the *Roland*. Oliver is on guard on a hill " Si veit venir cele gent paienur " (vs. 1019).

> Dist Oliver: 'Jo ai païens veüz:
> Unc mais nuls hom en tere n'en vit plus.
> Cil devant sunt .C. milie ad escuz,
> Helmes laciez e blancs obbercs vestuz;
> Dreites cez hanstes, luisent cil espiet brun.
> Bataille avrez, unches mais tel ne fut.
> Seigneurs Franceis, de Deu aiez vertut!
> El camp estez, que ne seium vencuz!'
> Dient Franceis: 'Dehet ait ki s'en fuit!
> Ja pur murir ne vous en faldrat uns.'  (vss. 1039-1048)

It is important to notice, however, Bodel's adaptation of this motif. Although in each case is presented a picture of the advancing Saracen army, dominated by the flashing of arms and armor (" Vés les armes reluire "; " Luisent cil espiet brun."), that of the *Roland* is an epic description while that of the *Jeu* has the emotional impact of a sudden outcry. The full line: " Vés le armes reluire: tous li cuers m'en esclaire " poetically conveys the immediate sensations of exhilaration and release in the hearts of the Christians, suddenly illuminated, as it were, by the flashing of enemy weapons.[7]

---

[7] Mario Roques, " Pour le commentaire d'Aucassin et Nicolette 'esclairier le cuer,' " *Mélanges d'histoire du moyen âge offerts à M. Ferdinand Lot* (Paris, 1925), pp. 723-736, examines numerous examples of the use of 'esclairier le cuer' and concludes: " Il faut donc conclure que la métaphore originelle n'est pas celle de la lumière répandue dans un cœur assombri; l'idée première est celle de 'mettre au net, nettoyer, dégager, débarrasser.' " (p. 730). Of Bodel's use of the phrase he says: " Si l'on entend: 'La lueur des armes illumine mon cœur,' il y aurait là un assez singulier concetto, d'autant plus étonnant qu'il s'agit des armes des Sarrasins. . . . Le combat qui s'annonce, c'est, pour les chrétiens que fait parler Jean Bodel, la fin des tribulations, des doutes, des peines. . . . C'est parce qu'ils vont être, 'fors de douleur' que les chrétiens se sentent le cœur *esclairié*, c'est-à-dire ici encore 'dégagé, libéré.' " (pp. 732-733). The evidence for this meaning of " esclairier le cuer " is overwhelming. Nevertheless, seeking support from Mario Roque's own statement: " Toutefois la coexistence dans *esclairier* des deux sens d' 'illuminer' et de 'nettoyer' aurait pu facilement fausser la valeur originelle de la formule *esclairier le cuer* et amener des Français du moyen âge à l'entendre . . . dans le sens d' 'illuminer l'âme' " (p. 732),

Bodel's Christians are sustained in the face of imminent calamity by the profound conviction that theirs will be a martyr's death and the recompense of Paradise. This is expressed by one of their number:

> Segneur, n'en doutés ja, vés chi vostre juïse:
> Bien sai tout i morrons el Damedieu serviche.   (vss. 401-402)
>
> Segnieur, el Dieu serviche soit hui chascuns offers!
> Paradys sera nostres et eus sera ynfers.   (vss. 405-406)

An angel appears to comfort the doomed warriors:

> Segneur, soiés tout aseür,
> N'aiés doutanche ne peür.
> Messagiers sui Nostre Segneur,
> Qui vous metra fors de doleur.
> Aiés vos cuers fers et creans
> En Dieu: ja pour ches mescreans
> Qui chi vous vienent abandon
> N'aiés les cuers se seürs non.
> Metés hardiement vos cors
> Pour Dieu, car chou est chi li mors
> Dont tout li pules morir doit
> Qui Dieu aime de cuer et croit.   (vss. 412-423)

The exhortation to knights about to engage in a particularly arduous battle to fight valiantly and the promise of eternal life are the two aspects of a constantly recurring motif in the *chansons de geste*. At moments of greatest peril this solemn encouragement is given in almost identical phrases. The following quotations from many sources show how Bodel has respected this epic tradition.

In the *Chanson de Roland* Archbishop Turpin assures the French before Roncevaux:

> ' Se vos murez, esterez seinz martirs,
> Sieges avrez el greignor pareis.'   (vss. 1134-1135)

During a lull in the battle he spurs on the hard-pressed knights, speaking not only as a messenger of God but as one of the martyrs:

> ' Seignors barons, n'en alez mespensant!
> Pur Deu vos pri que ne seiez fuiant,

---

it is submitted that Bodel's use of the phrase is to be read also in the sense of "La lueur des armes illumine mon cœur," an unusual *concetto* perhaps, but nonetheless poetic, and, moreover, particularly effective in the context of the sudden sight of Saracen arms.

> Que nuls prozdom malvaisement n'en chant.
> Asez est mielz que moerium cumbatant.
> Pramis nus est fin prendrum a itant,
> Ultre cest jurn ne serum plus vivant;
> Mais d'une chose vos soi jo ben guarant:
> Seint pareis vos est abandunant;
> As Innocenz vos en serez seant.'    (vss. 1515-1523)

In the *Chevalerie Vivien*[8] Vivien encourages his men at l'Archamp when they are somewhat dismayed by the awesome sight of the huge fleet bringing in Desramé and his army:

> Dist a ses homes: ' Bone gent asolue,
> N'aiés paor de la gent mescreüe
> Dont tant avés asanblee veüe.
> De rien se poine cil qui Deus nen aiue.
> Traions nos ça lés ceste roche agüe,
> Chascons restigne el poing l'espee nue;
> Qui ci mora, s'arme iert bien asolue,
> Avoc les anges servie et coneüe,
> En paradis avra maintes aües.
> Vers Damedeu ai covenance aiue
> Que ne fuirai por la gent mescreüe.'    (vss. 365-375)

Before leading the attack Vivien again addresses his men:

> ' Baron,' dist il, ' en Deu vos confortés.
> Dex nos a hui en son ciel apelés;
> Qui si mora ans ne fut si beur neis,
> El ciel sera ensanble les abés.'    (vss. 471-474)

The *chanson de geste Aquin*[9] which tells of Charlemagne's campaign in Brittany presents a remarkable series of battles and sieges and contains many such appropriate phrases of exhortation and divine promise. The Archbishop of Dol speaks:

> ' Pour Dieu, Seignours, no vous espargniez mie
> De bien feriz desus la gent haye,
> Qui cy mourra son ame soit requeillie
> En paradis en la Dieu compaignie! '    (vss. 560-564)

---

[8] *La chevalerie Vivien, chanson de geste*, ed. A.-L. Terracher (Paris, 1909).

[9] *Le roman d'Aquin ou la conqueste de la Bretaigne par le roy Charlemaigne, chanson de geste du XIIe siècle*, ed. F. Joüon des Longrais, SBB (Nantes, 1880).

The Duke of Naimes repeatedly encourages his men:

> ' Ferez chascus o l'espée tranchant
> Sus ces peans felons et mescreant!
> C'est tout pour Dieu, le pere omnipotent,
> Que nous soufron cest martire si grant;
> En paradis Damme Dé nous atant,
> Je ouay les anges qui cy nous vont querant
> De nous touz vont les armes attendant! ' (vss. 1569-1575)

> ' Barons,' dist il, ' ne soiez effrayé;
> C'est tout pour Dieu, le roy de majesté,
> Que nous soufron ceste fragilité;
> En paradis en seron couronné
> O les martirs et assis et posé!
> Ferez chascun o le branc acéré. . . .' (vss. 2459-2464)

In the *Couronnement de Louis*,[10] William, who has arrived at Rome as a pilgrim, takes command of the Pope's army to repel a Saracen invasion of Italy. The Pope makes a solemn declaration to the assembled combatants:

> ' Seignor baron,' dist l'apostoiles sages,
> Qui en cest jor morra en la bataille
> En paradis avra son herberjage,
> Que nostre sire a ses bons amis guarde;
> Sainz Gabrïels li sera guionages.' (vss. 426-430)

In *Aspremont*[11] the same theme of comfort, encouragement and exhortation to fight bravely with the promise of heavenly reward, frequently appears. Girard d'Eufrate, Charles's powerful ally in the Calabrian expedition, is told that Eaumont, son of the Saracen King Agolant, is returning to the attack with reinforcements to avenge his earlier defeat:

> Et dist Girars: ' Ne l'ai pas redotee.
> Franc chevalier, ves la cosse aprestée.
> De paradis est overte l'entree;
> Dex nos apele en sa joie honoree;
> Or sons venu a la sainte jornee.
> Cui Dex avra ici la mort donee
> De tant bone eure fu sa cars engenree.' (vss. 3885-3891)

---

[10] *Le Couronnement de Louis, chanson de geste du XII<sup>e</sup> siècle*, ed. Ernest Langlois, CFMA (Paris, 1920).

[11] *La chanson d'Aspremont, chanson de geste du XIIe siècle, texte du manuscrit de Wollaton Hall*, ed. Louis Brandin, CFMA, 2 vols. (Paris, 1919).

In similar fashion the Pope encourages the knights of Charlemagne when they come under attack:

> 'Ki or ira sor Sarrasins ferir
> Et le martire volra por Deu sofrir,
> Dex li fera paradis aovrir;
> La nos fera coroner et florir
> Et a sa destre nos fera aseïr.   (vss. 4304-4308)

Charlemagne in his turn exhorts his troops:

> 'Bon crestïen, or cevalciés avant.
> Paradis est overs des l'ajornant,
> La nos atendent li arcangle en cantant.'   (vss. 4402-4404)

It was not possible to represent on the stage the glorious vision of Paradise opening in the eastern sky, consequently Bodel was limited to introducing an angel to convey a promise of heavenly reward. Nevertheless, in the *chansons de geste,* such promises of Paradise, accompanying exhortations to fight bravely, are most often made by Pope or bishop, Emperor or Lord. Bodel, however, has an angel fulfill this function. Without here seeking the possible reasons for this departure from the tradition, it may be noted that the intervention of a divine personage in the affairs of the crusaders at moments of crisis is commonplace in the *chansons de geste.* Thus the assistance of the angel Gabriel is spoken of in the above quoted passage from the *Couronnement de Louis.* It will be recalled also that angels were present at the death of Roland, that Gabriel watched over Charlemagne as he slept after avenging Roland's defeat and also encouraged him in his fight with Baligant. Similarly, in *Fierabras,* an angel assures Charlemagne that Oliver will defeat his giant adversary. In *Aspremont,* Saints George, Dominique, and Mercury assist the French in the battle against Agolant, St. George being the special protector of Roland. The intervention of the Angel in the battle scene in the *Jeu,* then, is not in a true sense a departure from tradition; it serves, in fact, to strengthen the epic atmosphere of the episode and to underline the close relationship of the *Jeu* to the *chansons de geste.*

There remains for consideration the rôle of the *Crestïens nouviaus chevaliers* whose heroic words:

> Segneur, se je sui jones, ne m'aiés en despit!
> On a veü souvent grant cuer en cors petit.   (vss. 408-409)

call to mind, as Le Roy first pointed out,[12] the famous couplet of the Cid:

> Je suis jeune, il est vrai, mais aux âmes bien nées
> La valeur n'attend pas le nombre des années.

Jeanroy claims that here Bodel borrowed directly from *Fierabras*. In this *chanson de geste*, the Duke of Naimes makes a dramatic refusal when ordered to remain on guard while Roland and his fellow prisoners make a sortie in search of food from the tower they hold against their captor Balan in Aigremont:

> Rollans, li niés Karlon, a Namlon apelé;
> ' Sire, vous remanrés o Tieri l'aduré
> Por garder ceste porte tant k'estrons retorné.'
> ' Sire,' respont li dus, ' dont ai ge mal dehé,
> Se je suis vos portiers en trestout mon aé.
> Pour ce se je sui viex, ne m'aiés en vilté,
> Que je ai les ners durs et le cuer aceré.'   (vss. 3207-3213)

That the couplet of Bodel's young knight is reminiscent of the last couplet of Naimes' is undeniable but Jeanroy would seem to have over-emphasized their similarity. The likeness resides chiefly in the form of the first lines of the couplets, for despite the validity of the general observation that each of these persons is making a heroic claim and is concerned with his age, there is a distinct difference in content and in motive. It would not be true to say that the fear of the newly-dubbed knight of being despised on account of his youth echoes the feelings of the older knight. The difference in the underlying psychological situation belies such a conclusion. Bodel's knight is an untried youth anxious to prove his worth in battle. Naimes, on the other hand, is an old soldier with a long record of valor, not seeking to prove his worth but expressing violent resentment at being deprived of an opportunity to display it by being alloted a less dangerous task. This primary aspect of the Naimes episode is not uncommon in French heroic literature. In particular is it reminiscent of an episode in *Aspremont*. Soleman, the King of the Bretons, anticipating a violent clash with Eaumont, decides to send to Charlemagne for assistance. The knights Richier, Amauri, Godefroi, and Antelme in turn refuse to carry the message for fear of losing the honor of taking part in a particularly danger-

---

[12] Le Roy, p. 22.

ous encounter by accepting a comparatively safe mission (laisses 216-219). If the young knight in the *Jeu* is not the real counterpart of Naimes, he is, nonetheless, in a well-defined tradition of certain epic heroes. Not only is he newly-dubbed, young, small and determined to show himself equal in bravery to his elders, but he will do so by engaging in combat the strongest man in the opposing ranks. His words quoted above are immediately followed by:

> Je ferrai cel forcheur, je l'ai piecha eslit;
> Sachiés je l'ochirai, s'il anchois ne m'ochit.   (vss. 410-411)

He is to be recognized as an ideal hero evoking the great figures of Gui in the *Chanson de Guillaume*, Guichardés in *Chevalerie Vivien*, and Roland in *Aspremont*; he is also reminiscent of certain aspects of Oliver in *Fierabras*, and of William in the *Couronnement de Louis*.

When William is about to ride for l'Archamp a second time to avenge Vivien's defeat at the hands of Desramé and, considering the possibility of being killed in the battle, laments the lack of an heir, Gui, Vivien's young brother who " N'out uncore quinz anz, asez esteit petiz" (vs. 1441), declared he would assume that responsibility. In protesting William's brusque refusal he complains:

> ' Pur petitesce que m'avez a blasmer?
> Ja n'est nul si grant que petit ne fust né.'   (vss. 1464-1465)

William eventually accepts the boy as his heir, making the remark, " Cors as d'enfant e si as raisun de ber " (vs. 1479), which he repeats on two later occasions (vss. 1637, 1977). Gui is left behind when William sets out for l'Archamp and he weeps: " N'ai que quinze anz, si sui en tel vilté" (vs. 1517), and despite Guiborc's protest: " Trop par es enfes e de petit ée " (vs. 1526), persuades her to knight him so that he can follow William. Equipped with especially small arms and armour (laisse 127) Gui sets forth on Guiborc's horse. " Petit est Gui e li cheval est grant " (vs. 1553), but " Mielz portad armes que uns hom de trente anz" (vs. 1556). At l'Archamp he wins William's grudging sanction to remain with him with his pleading:

> ' Guidez vus dunc que Deus seit si oblié,
> Qui les granz homes pot tenir e garder,
> Qu'il ne face des petiz altretel?

> Ja n'est nul granz que petit ne fud né;
> Uncore hui ferrai de l'espee de mun lez,
> Si purrai ben mun hardement prover,
> Si en mei ert salvé l'onur e le herité!' (vss. 1651-1657)

Gui's persistence is rewarded and his knightly work finally recognized, for when the Saracens launch a surprise attack and even unhorse William, Gui comes to his rescue and fights so stoutly that the Saracens are put to flight, crying: " Revescuz est Vivien le guerreier!" (vs. 1854)

A similar story, though told in lesser detail, appears in *Chevalerie Vivien*. Here, Guichardés, Vivien's second brother, assumes the rôle of the eager youth. He, too, begs William to allow him to join the expedition to l'Archamp and he, too, is refused:

> 'Niés,' dist Guillelmes, 'ne vos removerés;
> Trop estes jones et de petit aei
> Por Sarrasins ferir et encontrer.' (vss. 1208-1210)

Again, after William's departure, does the nephew air his resentment at being left behind:

> Dist Guichardés: 'Or me puis aïrer,
> Que on me velt ceans anjeoleir.
> Assés suis grans por mes armes porter;
> Se ge demain, poi me doit on esmer.' (vss. 1289-1292)

Like Gui, he overcomes Guiborc's objections and sets out, a newly dubbed knight, to help his uncle. Proving himself by overcoming six Saracens on the way, he is accepted by William as a knight and takes his place in the battle of l'Archamp.

*Aspremont* offers in its turn the story of how Roland won his spurs. Faced with the necessity of leading an expedition to expel Agolant who has invaded Calabria, Charlemagne, although in dire need of all the men he can muster, is intent on preventing the four youths he has brought up, Roland, Athon, Estolt, and Guion, from joining him and has them confined at Laon:

> 'A cest besoing n'ai cure de garçon
> Ne d'espervier ne de vol d'oisellon,
> De nul deduit se de l'espee non.' (vss. 1062-1064)

Angered by this interdiction, the boys, under the leadership of Roland, escape from their prison by killing the jailer, and, stealing the horses of five Breton knights of King Salemon, they join the expedition, unknown to Charles. The French are hard-pressed in their first major battle and Charlemagne sends back to his camp for all men, combatants and non-combatants alike, to arm themselves as best they may and come to his assistance. It is Roland who organizes and instills a fierce ardor into this motley army and leads them to the battlefield where they are able to equip themselves with the arms and armor of fallen knights. We are reminded that Roland is not a knight, for as he equips himself from a dead Saracen

> Espee nuë ne degna il ballier,
> Car il n'ert mie encore chevalier,
> Mais il saisist a dos mains un levier;
> Uns fors vilains i eüst que ballier;
> Rollans ert jovenes mais fors estoit et fier.  (vss. 5548-5552)

Following Charlemagne closely, Roland rescues him from certain death at the hands of Eaumont and, although armed only with his "levier," which is now broken, he wins the admiration of the Saracen prince:

> 'Preus est cil gars et cuvers et estols.
> Li vif deable li ont doné tel tros
> Certes, s'il vit, molt iert cevaleros.'  (vss. 6036-6038)

Roland slays his adversary, who is no ordinary man, for, as Naimes says when subsequently reproaching Charles for venturing in solitary pursuit of this Saracen warrior:

> 'C'ert uns deables tos vis et enragié.
> Voiés quel teste et quel cors et quel pié.'  (vss. 6103-6104)

Despite this heroic feat, Roland has to plead with Charles to be knighted when the major battle against Agolant is imminent. Charles at first refuses:

> Et dist li rois: 'Ce fait bien a lascier.
> Rollans si est trop jovene a cest mestier.'  (vss. 7356-7357)

Nevertheless, the youth duly dubbed is given command of the first echelon of the French army, not without lingering misgivings on the part of Charles who orders Ogier to take care of his nephew:

> 'Ohi! Ogier, tenés moi covenant
> De mon neveu, por ce qu'il est enfant.'  (vss. 7805-7806)

Roland's first battle encounter as a knight is crowned with success for, although " Il fu petis et grans fu l'aversier " (vs. 8576), he dispatches in true epic fashion Mandaquin, considered by his fellow pagans the bravest and best knight in the world, and whose defeat so dismays them that they take flight saying of Roland: " Qui fu cel nain puant? " (vs. 8614)

Throughout the ensuing battle Roland, with the special help of St. George, maintains the same pitch of enthusiasm and courage and is largely responsible for the ultimate success of the Christian cause. Well and truly does he prove his worth as a knight despite his inexperience, youth, and smallness of stature.

Oliver in *Fierabras* and William in *Couronnement de Louis*, although no longer untried knights, also show certain aspects of this ideal type of heroism. Each faces and fights in single combat the strongest man in the Saracen ranks. Oliver, though suffering from severe wounds, volunteers with the greatest eagerness to fight the powerful giant Fierabras — " En son estant puet on XV piés measurer " (vs. 575) — when not one Frenchman dares accept the giant's challenge and even Roland most violently refuses. William kills in single combat an equally fearsome Saracen, Corsolt, " Le plus fort ome dont on oïst parler " (vs. 311). During this fight, Corsolt, reeling beneath the first blow, exclaims:

> ' Molt par est fols qui petit ome blasme,
> Quant il le veit entrer en grant bataille.'   (vss. 923-924)

Of such stuff is the *Crestïens nouviaus chevaliers* made, and his appearance in Bodel's play, brief though it is, was undoubtedly sufficient to conjure up in the minds of the audience the spirit and deeds of many familiar figures in the gallery of epic heroes.[13]

---

[13] It is instructive to compare this motif to the literary topos *puer-senex* treated by E. R. Curtius in " Knabe und Greis," *Europäische Literatur und Lateinisches Mittelalter* (Bern, 1948), pp. 106-109. Although the epic figure of the young knight, brave and strong beyond his years, possesses, as in the case of Guy in the *Chanson de Guillaume*, mental faculties of a mature man (three times does William say to him: " Cors as d'enfant e si as raisun de ber "), it is not primarily this aspect which gives him heroic stature. On the other hand, the many examples quoted by Curtius from Classical and Late Latin authors, the Bible and the Church Fathers, etc., show the *puer-senex* to be primarily a youth distinguished by the wisdom and prudence of a grown man. The type of hero under discussion above would seem to belong to another tradition, equally ancient and a manifesta-

The phase of Bodel's miracle play dealing with the calling of the King of Africa's subjects to arms to meet the Christian invasion is the counterpart of the initial mustering of troops in *Aspremont*. In the epic, however, the mobilization is of the Christian forces of Charlemagne to expel the Saracen invaders from his territory. Nevertheless, despite this basic transposition, similarities in situation, action, and phraseology are strikingly apparent.

To throw back the Christian aggressors the King of Africa sends far and wide, most urgently demanding assistance. To his messenger Auberon he issues these instructions:

> Auberon, au bien courre soies entalentiex.
> Va moi par tout semonre Gaians et Queneliex.
> Moustre par tout mes lettres et mon seel apert,
> Comment par crestïens ma loys dechiet et pert.
> Chil qui demou[e]rront soient seür et chiert
> Qu'il et leur oir seront a tous jours mais cuivert.
> Va t'en, je te cuidoie ja dehors le banlieue.   (vss. 241-247)

The same expression of outrage at suffering invasion and the same threat against those vassals who refuse assistance are present in Charles' address to his assembled barons:

> ' Franc chevalier,' dist Carles al barnage,

---

tion, overlapping but not identical with, the tradition of the *puer-senex*, of the universal collective subconscious, the David and Goliath topos, in which the emphasis is on the courage of the youth in fighting a giant adversary. In support of this view may be quoted the legend attributed to Notker Balbulus, as to the origin of the significant surname of Pépin le Bref. Gaston Paris in " La légende de Pépin ' le Bref,' " *Mélanges de littérature française du moyen âge*, pub. Mario Roques (Paris, 1912), pp. 103-215, gives the following account of the legend: " Pépin sachant que les principaux chefs francs le méprisent (évidemment à cause de sa petite taille), fait amener un taureau et un lion, et, quand le lion a renversé le taureau et va le dévorer, il descend seul de son trône, au milieu de la terreur de tous les assistants, et tranche d'un coup d'épée la tête des deux animaux féroces; puis, s'adressant aux grands stupéfaits: ' Croyez-vous, leur dit-il, que je puisse être votre maître? N'avez-vous pas entendu raconter ce que le petit David a fait à l'immense Goliath ou le tout petiti (brevissimus) Alexandre à ses gigantesques compagnons? '." The tale concerning Alexander is unknown, but it presumably would exemplify the same topos. L. Spitzer, " Etudes d'anthroponymie ancienne française: II, Pépin ' le Bref,' " *PMLA*, LVII (1943), 593-596, supports the view that " le surnom *Pippinus Brevis* et l'histoire de la petitesse de taille de ce roi découlent du sens originaire du nom propre qui signifiait à l'origine ' petit.' "

> ' Esgardés ore quel honte et quel damage
> Ont fait sor moi la pute gens salvage
> Qui sont issu et d'Alfrique et d'Arrage
> Et arivé en mon droit iretage.
> Venes od moi en cest pelerinage.
> Qui n'i venra n'i metra altre gage;
> Culvers sera et il et son linage.' (vss. 864-871)

Here may be introduced the second comparison made by Jeanroy between the *Jeu* and *Fierabras*. Auberon's reply to the above quoted words of the King is:

> Sire, n'en doutés ja, nus cameus une lieue
> N'est tant isniaus de courre que je na raconsieue,
> Derrier moi ne le meche devant demie lieue. (vss. 248-250)

In *Fierabras* Balan sends his dragoman on an urgent mission:

> Et dist li drugemans: ' Bien li sarai conter;
> Mais n'i voel dromadaire pour cevaucer mener,
> En I jour en vauroie XIIII trespasser;
> Ja pour C lieues courre ne me verrés lasser' (vss. 4277-4280)

Just as the King of Africa sends his messenger with letters and his seal to the great vassals of his empire, the Emirs of Orkenie, Coine, Oliferne, and Outre le Sec Arbre, so does Charlemagne send messengers with letters to the kings of his empire, Cahoër of England, Gondelbuef the Frisian, Brunols of Hungary, Salemon of Brittany, Droon of Manseis, Anseïs of Cologne, and David of Cornwall, announcing the invasion and requesting their assistance. Emirs and kings alike respond immediately to the royal summons with promises of men and, in some cases, of treasure. Among the emirs, Coine promises: " Je li menrai riche conroi " (vs. 319); Sec Arbre: " Vous menrai cent mile paiens " (vs. 338). Orkenie announces upon his arrival: ". . . je vous fac venir par mer / Cent navees de mon tresor " (vss. 365-366); and Oliferne: ". . . je vous amain trente cars / Plains de rubis et d'esmeraudes " (vss. 371-372). As for Charlemagne's kings, each promises ten thousand men and, in addition, Cahoër's men

> En un dromont qu'a Dovre font cargier
> D'or et d'argent et de fier et d'achier
> Entrent trestolt et prendent a nagier. (vss. 909-911)

Gondelbuef, like Coine, says:

> ' Se li menrai un si riche conroi
> Qui Sarrasins feront duel et anoi.' (vss. 932-933)

Droon of Mansois also leads a powerful force to join Charlemagne:

> A dis milliers, a molt riches conrois
> Passent la mer a force et a desrois. (vss. 969-970)

In adapting to his own use the embassy of Charlemagne in *Aspremont,* Bodel exhibits once again his ability to treat in an original fashion the material he has transposed. Here it is cast into a distinctive form particularly suitable for dramatic representation on the multiple stage. Scene V, concerning the visit to the four Emirs, is a masterpiece of dramatic-lyric parallelism and presents a series of ballet-like cadenzas. Auberon approaches the Emir of Coine and addresses him:

> Mahom saut l'amiral del Coine,
> De par le roy, qui sans essoigne
> Li mande qu'en s'aïe viegne! (vss. 315-317)

The Emir replies:

> Auberon, che me di au roy:
> Je li menrai riche conroi,
> N'iert essoigne qui me retiegne. (vss. 318-320)

Auberon retires and approaches the Emirs of Orkenie and Oliferne, each time the same stylized pattern being repeated in the salutation in the name of Mahomet, the royal summons, and the anxious assurance of all possible help, the regularly rhymed sextet used for each "audience" being divided equally between the ambassador and the emir. The rhythmic motion and the formal flourish of gesture accompanying each courtly visit can well be imagined. The delivery of the summons to the Emir of Outre le Sec Arbre stands in interesting contrast, however, bringing the scene to a noticeably humorous conclusion. As we learn later, this emir, unlike his peers, is exceedingly poor—millstones are the currency in his country and he can bring the King no gifts—and he is presumably less highly respected than the others, at least by Auberon. Auberon accordingly approaches him without ceremony, omits the formal salutation and demands his help not, as before, "de par le roy," but as if to show awareness of the humble circumstances of the Emir, in the name of a powerful monarch. Taking four lines of the sextet it will be noted, Auberon speaks:

> Amiraus d'outre le Sec Arbre,
> Li roys d'Aïr, Tranle et Arabe

> Pour le guerre des crestïens
> Te mande le secours prochain. (vss. 333-336)

In the Emir's reply, direct, practical, and loyal, is to be seen a pleasingly humorous scorn of the servile boasts of his opulent peers and a subtle rebuke to the presumptuous Auberon:

> Auberon, le matin bien main
> Vous menrai cent mile paiens. (vss. 337-338)

Since the issue of the crusade in the *Jeu*, unlike the historical crusades, is religious rather than political, involving the conversion of a Saracen country to Christianity rather than its physical conquest, and since the Saracen of medieval literature is distinguished chiefly by his supposed religious practices, it is not surprising to find that the action of the scenes laid in the African court revolves largely around the Saracen gods and the attitude of the King and vassals towards them. Tervagant, as an idol, is a central figure in these scenes and although *Mahom* and *Apolin* do not appear as idols, frequent oaths and allusions to them do not allow us to forget that they are the other gods of the trio usually associated with the Saracen faith. This trio is frequently mentioned in *chansons de geste*, often appearing as idols, as in the *Roland, the Siège de Barbastre*,[14] *Floovant*,[15] and in *Aspremont*, and even when other gods are mentioned such as Jupiter, Cahu, and Margot, it is the first mentioned trio which predominates.[16]

Tervagant is introduced in the opening scene of the play as the butt of the King's wrath when he learns of the Christian invasion:

> A! fiex a putain, Tervagan,
> Avés vous dont souffert tel œuvre?
> Com je plaing l'or dont je vous cuevre
> Che lait visage et che lait cors!
> Certes, s'or ne m'aprent mes sors
> Les crestïens tous a confondre,
> Je vous ferai ardoir et fondre

---

[14] *Le siège de Barbastre, chanson de geste du XIIe siècle*, ed. J. L. Perrier, CFMA (Paris, 1926).

[15] *Floovant, chanson de geste du XIIe siècle, publiée avec introduction, notes et glossaire, thèse pour le doctorat*, Sven Andolf (Uppsala, 1941).

[16] For the provenance of the names of these Saracen divinities see L. Sainéan, *Les sources indigènes de l'étymologie française* (Paris, 1925), II, 430-437, 448.

>     Et departir entre me gent;
>     Car vous avés passé argent
>     S'iestes du plus fin or d'Arrabe. (vss. 134-143)

The Seneschal is shocked by the King's angry outburst:

>     A roys! Ne. l deüssiés pas dire
>     Tel outrage ne tel desroi. (vss. 146-147)

He urges him to undo the possible damage done to the Saracen cause:

>     Alons a Tervagan andoi
>     Prier qu'il ait pardon de nous,
>     A nus keutes, a nus genous,
>     Si que par sa sainte vertu
>     Soient crestïen abatu. (vss. 152-156)

The god is to be placated and his good offices sought with gifts:

>     Et si prometés Tervagan
>     Dis mars d'or a croistre ses joes. (vss. 162-163)

As Jeanroy observes, this incident is very similar to an episode in *Fierabras*. Balan is enraged at Charlemagne's easy penetration of his outlying defenses and, betraying the instability of character typical of the *mescreant*, furiously assails with curses his god, Mahomet, and beats him with a cudgel.[17] The great vassals of the royal entourage are shocked by their sovereign's behavior and persuade him to make amends to the idol:

>     De Mahonz s'aprocha, envers lui s'umelie.
>     Tant ont prié Balant li paiens Sortinbras
>     Et li niés Tempesté, Cordroés et Brulans,
>     K'i li a amendé de .XX^m. besans;
>     De tant li fera croistre les costés et les flans. (vss. 5172-5176)

This incident is not the only reminiscence of the *chansons de geste* in the opening scene of the *Jeu*. The whole atmosphere created by details of the description of the idol and the King's attitude toward Tervagant is redolent of traditional Saracen scenes in the epics, in particular the *Siège de Barbastre*, remarkable for the richness of its "Saracen" coloring.

---

[17] This typical irascibility of the *mescreant* may be observed not only among the Saracen monarchs of the epics, but it is also characteristic of the figure of Herod in the many liturgical plays of medieval times concerning the Coming of the Magi and the Slaughter of the Innocents (Young, *Drama*, II, 33-124).

In this *chanson de geste* the Emir of Spain, like the King of Africa in the *Jeu*, prays to his idol for his assistance in the fight against the Christians:

> 'Mahomet, sire, que demores tu tant?
> Venge moi des François, par itel covenant
> Que de trois mile mars d'or fin arrabiant
> Vos croistrai les costez et les flans par devant.'
> (vss. 1485-1488)

The King in the *Jeu* requests in his prayer to Tervagant a sign whereby the outcome of the conflict with the Christians shall be known. The idol both smiles and weeps and it falls to the Seneschal to interpret this sign for the King. Similarly, in the epic, Mahomet answers the Emir of Spain's prayer with a sign which the Emir's chief adviser, the governor of Cordova, interprets:

> 'Mahom est corrociez, jeu voi a escïent;
> Veez conme li oil li vont estancelant,' (vss. 1491-1492)

The device of the oracle and its interpretation is, in the *Jeu*, much more humorous than in the *Siège de Barbastre*. The grotesque irascibility of the King and the servile but cunning character of the Seneschal are amusingly displayed in the King's abject posturing before the idol, the unwillingness of the Seneschal to explain the idol's sign for fear of the wrath of his royal master, his extraction of the promise that he will not suffer for his explanation of the oracle and the king's furious outburst when the ominous meaning is finally made clear to him and the Seneschal, by virtue of the promise, is safe from his spiteful anger.

Receiving the news of the arrival of reinforcements, the Emir duly shows his gratitude to his gods:

> L'amirant ot le mes, si mercie Apolin;
> Mahom en a gagié plus de mil mars d'or fin. (vss. 5476-5477)

When the tide of battle turns against him, the Emir calls upon Mahomet to turn back the French with further promises of gold:

> 'Hé! Mahomet!' dit il, 'tornez les a hontage.
> Dont ne voiz tu conment iceste gent s'enrage,
> Qui ma gent ont ocise l'orgueil et le fiertaje?
> De quatre cenz mars d'or te croistrai ton omage.'
> (vss. 5532-5535)

The Emir's affairs do not prosper and, like the King of Africa, he resorts to abuse of his god:

> Li amirant d'Espangne si l'a forment laidi:
> 'Mauvés dieu non poisant, con estes endormiz!
> Que feroiz de Francois? Gasté ont mon païs
> Et mes citez sessies et mes homes ocis.' (vss. 6117-6120)

The Emir's fortunes go from bad to worse and soon Louis of France is in a position to demand his surrender. The Emir is so incensed that he threatens his idol with destruction:

> 'Mahomet, dit il, sire, tu soies vergongnié,
> Se demein n'est par toi li domajes venchiez;
> Autresin con cist est seras tu vergongniez:
> Je te ferai brisier et la teste et les piez,
> Puis seras con un chien en un fossé lanciez.'
> (vss. 6516-6520)

The final scene of the *Jeu* closes with the humiliation and destruction of the idol Tervagant. The King orders the Seneschal to throw him down and the Seneschal obeys with alacrity. This climax is in keeping with the general course of pagan affairs in the *chansons de geste*. Almost invariably the Saracens, when finally defeated, with varying degrees of violence renounce and destroy their gods, carrying out, in fact, such threats as those quoted above uttered by the King and the Emir of Spain. Such episodes easily lend themselves to dramatization and it is possible to imagine that Tervagant's sorry end was fully exploited by actors of Bodel's play who would give full expression to the grotesque pantomime inspired by such well-known scenes from the epics as the violent end of the Saracen gods in the *Roland* at the hands of Marsilie and his followers:

> Ad Apolin en curent en une crute,
> Tencent a lui, laidement le despersunent:
> 'E! malvais deus, por quei nus fais tel hunte?
> Cest nostre rei por quei lessas cunfundre?
> Ki mult te sert, malvais leur l'en dunes!'
> Puis si li tolent sun sceptre e sa curune,
> Par les mains le pendent sur une columbe,
> Entre lur piez a tere le tresturnent,
> A granz bastuns le batent e defruisent;
> E Tervagan tolent sun escarbuncle
> E Mahumet enz en un fosset butent
> E porc e chen le mordent e defulent. (vss. 2580-2591)

The almost matter of fact conversion of pagans to Christianity when finally subdued in battle is another characteristic of the *chansons de geste* faithfully reproduced in the *Jeu de saint Nicolas*. One apparently dissenting note, however, is the unwillingness of the Emir of Orkenie to follow the lead of his king and peers:

> A! rois, pour Mahommet, merchi!
> Ne me fai mes diex renoier!
> Fai me anchois le teste soier
> Ou mon cors a cheval detraire!    (vss. 1506-1509)

He yields only to violent physical compulsion and cries out with spirit:

> Sains Nicolais, c'est maugré mien
> Que je vous aoure et par forche;
> De moi n'arés vous fors l'escorche:
> Par parole devieng vostre hom
> Mais li creanche est en Mahom.    (vss. 1512-1516)

Jeanroy sees this episode ("assez incongru et parfaitement inutile") as certainly based on the dénouement of *Fierabras*. Balan finally yields to the persuasion of Fierabras and Floripas and agrees to be baptized. At the last moment, however, he gives vent to a fit of rage, spits into the holy water and strikes the bishop. To waste no further time, Augier unceremoniously cuts off his head. Despite Jeanroy's assertion to the contrary, Bodel's episode is of value in the play. It provides the action necessary to relieve the monotony of an otherwise uneventful and banal situation and adds considerably to the characterization. Orkenie shows considerable strength of character, for in remaining faithful to his gods he at first vigorously refuses to obey the King's command to embrace Christianity and even threatens his sovereign lord:

> Fourfait as c'on t'arde ou escorche!
> Toi ne ton savoir ne te forche
> Ne pris mais vaillant un espi.
> Garde de moi, je te deffi,
> Et renc ton hommage et ton fief.    (vss. 1489-1493)

The supposition that Bodel's audience would appreciate the representation of this untoward occurrence in a scene of conversion and would bestow at least gruding admiration upon Orkenie would seem to be well-founded, for again can it be shown that Bodel is utilizing an epic situation and recreating an epic character. Just as the

*Crestïens nouviaus chevaliers* represents a certain type of Christian hero, so is Orkenie in the tradition of a certain type of Saracen hero. Although, in the epic, no Saracen, unless he renounces his faith, can come to a good end, there also exists the Saracen who is brave, strong, true to his faith, in no way a coward; in short, a worthy opponent of the noblest knight of Christendom. It is of such a warrior that the jongleur frequently says, as in the *Roland*, when Baligant is described:

> Deus! quel baron, s'oüst chrestientet! (vss. 3164)

Oliver's opponent Fierabras, is of the same type:

> Se il vausist créir le digne roi Jhesu,
> N'éust tel chevalier dusques à Montagu. (vss. 582-583)

So it is with Balan in *Fierabras*. Although the extreme disrespect he shows at the moment of baptism damns him as a villain, his fanatical adherence to his faith has its admirable quality and his death by the sword is a martyrdom. A further example of this type of Saracen hero, unmarred, moreover, by villainous traits, is the great Saracen King Agolant in *Aspremont*. Throughout the epic he is drawn more sympathetically than his son Eaumont and maintains his dignity and steadfastness of religious faith even in crushing defeat. His army almost entirely destroyed and his horse killed under him, Agolant's position is hopeless. Girars d'Eufrate gives him the chance to surrender:

> A Agolant envoie un latimier:
> 'Se il voloit Mahomet renoier
> Et saint batesme et prendre et otroier,
> Par ce poroit bien sa vie aslongier
> Et rices teres avroit a justicier.' (vss. 10452-10456)

Bristling with pride, the King spurns the offer:

> Dist Agolans: 'Fui de ci, paltonier.
> Tu n'ies pas om que je doie tochier.
> Ne te caut mie de moi a aproismier,
> Car tu avroies ja endroit ton loier.
> Ja en ma tere ne lairai novelier,
> Ne mes lignages n'en avra reprovier
> Que par paor me face baptissier.
> Mels vuel morir que Damerdeu proier.' (vss. 10458-10465)

There is but one possible consequence. Claire, Girars' nephew, rushes in and, after a brief struggle, kills the unyielding Saracen:

> Claires a trait le brant forbi d'achier;
> Agolant fiert un grant cop et plenier
> A mont en l'elme desus le capelier.
> Prist ent la teste a l'espee d'acier.    (vss. 10479-10482)

This investigation into the relationship between the *Jeu de saint Nicolas* and the *chansons de geste* supports the view advanced earlier that this miracle play contains a story largely made up of commonplaces from the Old French epics. In addition to the reminiscences of *Fierabras* noted by Jeanroy, it shows similarities to most of the *chansons* of the Charlemagne and William of Orange cycles. In drawing upon the epics, Bodel was utilizing material familiar to him as a jongleur, but the story he constructed must not be regarded merely as a *pastiche*, a literary *tour de force*. The scenes, motifs, situations, personages, and phraseology must have had a profound effect on his audiences, strongly evoking for them episodes and figures of the many well-known *chansons de geste* and the whole complex of popular epic traditions. The great impression this background would convey would be one of great familiarity and it would be so much in keeping with the general taste and popular imagination shaped by two hundred years of *chansons de geste*, told and retold, as to be readily acceptable as a setting for the rehabilitation of an out-moded legend.

The appeal of this aspect of the *Jeu*, however, does not depend entirely upon the universal popularity and familiarity of the *chansons de geste* seem only as epic poems of heroism and faith. The epics were a true product of their age, a constant reminder of the Saracen threat to Christendom and of the glorious lot of the Christian soldier: they both expressed and stimulated the crusading spirit of the twelfth century. Similarly, if we are to regard the *Jeu de saint Nicolas* as the expression of a facet of medieval life, we must recognize in it traces of the same spirit which gave vitality to the *chansons de geste*. The epic scenes embodied in it, then, are not altogether formal copies of the *chansons* but are, to some extent, the direct expression and the gratification of the emotions deeply stirred by crusading events and echo, albeit faintly, the Church's exhortations to take the Cross. Thus the suitability of the setting for the new representation of the legend of St. Nicholas becomes even more evident when we consider the appeal to the patriotic and religious fervor so often at its peak during the century and at the time of the composition of the *Jeu* roused to new heights by the preparations for the Fourth Crusade. This crusading zeal was, moreover, particularly strong in Arras at the turn of the century. The capital city of Artois, it lies in the center of Picardy, which under Baudoin IX of Flanders provided, with Champagne under Thibaut III, the majority of the forces which set out for the crusade of 1202, vigorously advocated by Pope Innocent III and eloquently preached by Foulques de Neuilly. Both Villehardhouin [18] and Robert de Clari [19] in their respective accounts of the preparations for the Fourth Crusade, although not pretending to give exhaustive lists, in giving the names of those who took the Cross with the Count of Flanders at Bruges, mention, as far as can be judged, most of the important communes north of the Somme and east of the Scheldt. Particularly does Robert de Clari, who names crusaders of high and low estate, leave us with the impression of an overwhelming response in Artois to the call to the crusade. He concludes his long introductory list of those who took the Cross: " Et chiaus que nous avons ichi nommés, che furent chil qui plus y fisent d'armes et de proesches; et molt d'autre boine gent a cheval et a pié, tant de milliers que nous n'en savons le nombre " (p. 4). For information as to the men of Arras who joined the crusade we may turn to Bodel's *Congiés*,[20] a moving farewell to Arras when, stricken by leprosy, the poet was about to retire to a leper colony. The constantly recurring theme is Bodel's regret at not being able to fulfill his crusader's vows. Many of the friends of whom he movingly takes leave have, we are told, taken the Cross: Simon Disier, Waast Hukedeu, Robert Piedargentinois, Baud and Thomas, Renaut de Bieauvais, Waignet, and Nicoles li Carpentiers.

The crusading element of the *Jeu de saint Nicolas* is to be seen both as an elaboration of familiar, evocative themes and features of the *chansons de geste* which held the key to the imagination of

[18] Villehardhouin, *La conquête de Constantinople*, ed. and trans. E. Faral (Paris, 1939), pp. 1 ff.

[19] Robert de Clari, *La conquête de Constantinople*, ed. Philippe Lauer, CFMA (Paris, 1924), pp. 1 ff.

[20] " Les congés de Jean Bodel," ed. G. Raynaud, *Rom.*, IX (1880), 217-247. Reprinted in *Mélanges de philologie romane* (Paris, 1913), pp. 276-314.

Bodel's contemporaries, and as an expression of and offering to the crusading spirit which was particularly strong in Artois in the years immediately preceding the Fourth Crusade. It is not, indeed, a mere hors d'œuvre [21] preceding the so-called realistic tavern element, but—and in this it is equally realistic—an inevitable background and setting for the presentation of a traditional church legend in modern, lay, popular form, and an essential ingredient in a poetic expression of the attitude of the twelfth century Arras citizen towards a popular saint.

---

[21] " Cependant tout jusq'ici n'a été que hors-d'œuvre."  Lintilhac, p. 254.

## CHAPTER IV

### THE TAVERN

If the crusading element of the *Jeu de saint Nicolas* appealed to the epic-nourished imagination and to the religious and patriotic emotions of the people of Arras, then the realistic scenes centering around the actions of the thieves who steal the King's treasure appealed to their less exalted appetites and to a good-humored appreciation of the low-life of their city. Although the setting of the play is ostensibly an unnamed Saracen country somewhere in the empire of the King of Africa, these scenes of low-life, as will be shown, are purely Arrasian. Directly observed from life and with fantasy and exaggeration playing but a small part, they afforded the onlookers the enjoyment of seeing themselves as in a mirror. In all probability the characters were recognizable not merely as well-known types but as living persons of Arras and this, with an abundance of other local and topical allusion, whose full savor is unfortunately lost to us, conspired to lend the simple story a racy familiarity counterbalancing and complementing the more spiritual and more poetically evocative elements of the play.

Simple though it is, the story woven around the incidents taking place or originating in the tavern merits study, for besides its intrinsic worth as a vehicle for amusing dialogue and the importance of its local color as a background for the miracle, it is essential, as will be seen later, to the development and unity of the threads of the action culminating in the miracle. This three-fold value resides not merely in an expansion of the rôle of the thieves of the traditional legend; the tavern itself is all-important, and with the part played by the Tavernkeeper — and to some extent that of his assistant—gave Bodel a greater opportunity for presenting comic situations, humorous exchanges, true-to-life characters and other realistic elements of the Arras scene and also the means of bringing together and integrating the initially divergent aspects of the plot, now exotic and lofty, now familiar and low.

The story begins with the Tavernkeeper standing at the door of his inn, trying to attract customers by calling out the merits of the food and drink his establishment has to offer. Although in a hurry to carry out his duty as the King's messenger, Auberon, passing by, is tempted to stop for refreshment. An argument develops over the price of the wine and at the Tavernkeeper's suggestion Auberon accepts the offer of a game of dice made by another customer, Cliquet, the stake being the price of the drink. Auberon wins and goes on his way. Perturbed by the slowness of his business, the Tavernkeeper sends his potboy, Caignet, to get Raoulet, a town crier, to cry his wine. After an argument with Connart, a second crier, who has just called the King's proclamation, inviting anyone who so wished to steal the unguarded and unlocked royal treasure, Raoulet carries out the innkeeper's commission. Another passerby, Pincedé, attracted by the lyrical praise of the wine, enters and is greeted by Cliquet as an old drinking companion. Just as they are settling down to drink, much to the disgust of Caignet, who knows they have no money, the third rogue, Rasoir, enters and lavishly orders wine, explaining his unwonted extravagance by telling them of the King's *ban* concerning his treasure to which they can help themselves as soon as it is dark enough. Until the moment for carrying out their scheme arrives they drink and dice and quarrel. When the time comes to set out they take the landlord into their confidence and he, assured of a share in the loot, promises them the use of his inn for their and the treasure's shelter. The theft is duly accomplished without difficulty and, returning to the warm welcome of the innkeeper—fire, chairs, candles in plenty, and the best wine—the thieves embark upon a long dice game. Eventually, exhausted by wine and quarreling, they yield to sleep, intending to share their spoils later. St. Nicholas, however, rudely awakens them and terrifies them into returning the stolen treasure. The Tavernkeeper, anxious to get rid of the thieves, ostensibly fearing the loss of reputation for abetting a robbery, has Caignet eject them and has to be satisfied with Cliquet's cloak as payment of the score. Stifling a last temptation to keep at least some of the treasure for themselves, the thieves replace it and go their separate ways, each, undaunted by their unfortunate experience, already intent upon a theft he has in mind.

The vigorous realism of these tavern scenes and of the characters portrayed in them has long been fully recognized and the observation in the introduction and in the notes to Warne's edition of the play would seem to offer the last word in comment on this facet of the *Jeu*, always allowing for the possible discovery of corroborative documentary detail concerning the social life and customs in medieval Arras and for inevitable differences of opinion in the appreciation and interpretation of the less obvious humorous situations and exchanges. As this most recent editor says, with some regret, " we doubtless miss much of what his [Bodel's] audience appreciated in piquancy and sly allusion " (p. xviii). But if the presentation of a new view of the play based on the unity of its various features necessitates a repetition of what has often been well treated in detail, it affords the opportunity to gather and to synthesize much of what has heretofore been expressed by many critics in many places. Moreover, since our interest is not here primarily in the documentary value of these scenes as yielding precious information concerning the manners and customs of the Arras of Bodel's day but rather in the literary aspect of their realism, it is possible, in attempting to analyze their contribution to the artistic integrity of the play, to take full account of the realism of the characters who, undoubtedly drawn from life, may well be discussed by the literary critic seeking evidence of poetic expression if not by the historian seeking documentary material.

The first Arrasian scene opens, as we have said, with the Tavern-keeper standing at the door shouting to attract customers:

>  Chaiens fait bon disner, chaiens!
>  Chi a caut pain et caus herens
>  Et vin d'Aucheurre a plain tonnel.    (vss. 251-253)

Outside the inn we may imagine a prominently displayed wine-cask hoop, the distinguishing mark of the tavern in medieval Arras, for Auberon, arriving upon the scene, exclaims: " A! saint Beneoit, vostre anel / Me laissiés encontrer souvent! " (vss. 254-255).[1] In standing outside his establishment calling out its attractions, the

---

[1] " Cet anneau de saint Benoit . . . est simplement un cercle de tonneau, cercle 'béni' des voyageurs altérés, qui servit longtemps d'enseigne aux marchands de vins d'Arras." A. Guesnon, " Trouvères artésiens," *MA*, XXI (1908), 74. Evidence of this practice is to be found in Arras archives: " Un arrêt du parlement du 31 mars 1424 v. st. ordonne une enquête au sujet du préjudice causé à la ville d'Arras par ceux qui, pour frauder les droits, *in domibus suis vina, cerevisias et alia pocula absque intersignis, circulis et foliis ad potos et assietam vendebant* (Arch. comm. d'Arras)." (p. 74, note 1).

landlord is following a usual medieval practice,[2] other literary examples of which are to be found in the *fabliau, Des trois avugles de Compiègne,* by Cortebarbe,[3] and in *Courtois d'Arras*.[4] Late, in a further effort to improve his trade, the Tavernkeeper sends Caignet to tell Raoulet to cry his wine for him:

> Caignet, nous vendons mout petit.
> Va, se di Raoul que il crit
> Le vin; le gent en sont saoul.   (vss. 591-593)

Before entering the inn, Auberon is careful to enquire as to the quality and price of the wine vaunted by the Tavernkeeper. This seems to have been the usual precaution when entering a strange tavern; Courtois, too, observes it.[5] The inference is that tavernkeepers of the time were as likely as not to cheat the customer, a tendency indicated by the reply of Bodel's innkeeper to Auberon's questions:

> Au ban de le ville.
> Je n'en serai a nul fourfait
> Ne du vendre ne du mestrait.[6]   (vss. 258-260)

Whether the Tavernkeeper has a guilty conscience or is merely showing an awareness of the tendency to sharp practice among his kind, some such preoccupation is obvious from this hasty assurance that he neither overcharges nor gives short measure. Moreover, the very existence of municipal control indicated by the phrase " au ban de le vile " underlines the necessity for care in dealing with tavernkeepers.[7] Auberon's remark about the smallness of his tankard might be taken as a further expression of mistrust: " Chis hanas n'est mie parfons, / Il fust bons a vin assaier " (vss. 270-271).

---

[2] Monmerqué et Michel, *Théâtre,* p. 166, note.

[3] *Cortebarbe. Les trois avugles de Compiègne, fabliau du XIIIe siècle,* ed. Georges Gougenheim, *CFMA* (Paris, 1932), vss. 69-77.

[4] *Courtois d'Arras, jeu du XIIIe siècle,* ed. Edmond Faral, 2nd ed. rev. *CFMA* (Paris, 1922), vss. 103-113.

[5] *Courtois d'Arras,* vss. 126-127.

[6] " I shall not defraud (be guilty towards) anyone about it either in respect of selling (i. e. overcharging) or of short measure " (Warne's translation, p. 73, note to vss. 257-260).

[7] " In the Middle Ages the price of wine was fixed in towns and overcharging was punishable; many churches have sculptures and carvings showing innkeepers being punished in the fires of Hell for overcharging or for short measure " (Warne, p. 73, note to vs. 258).

This lingering suspicion would seem to be well founded, for when the messenger comes to pay for his wine, it becomes apparent that the seemingly innocent and assuring " au ban de le vile " is a trap. The actual price of the wine, carefully not mentioned before, is such that, each *pinte* costing three-quarters of a *denier*, it is up to the customer either to drink a second *pinte* and pay one and a half *denier*s or to pay a full *denier* for the first *pinte* and to leave, with the doubtful assurance of a second, at some later date, for half a *denier*, or *maille*; it is evident both here and in later reckonings that the quarter *denier* or *parti* did not exist at this time as a coin and that the smallest piece of currency was the *maille*.[8] The Tavernkeeper's trickery in this transaction is clearly exposed in the very readiness of his reply to Auberon's question as to how much he owed for his *pinte*; with no explanation or hesitation, now that the wine has been consumed, he firmly demands:

> Paie denier et a l'autre eure
> Aras le pinte pour maaille;
> C'est a douze deniers sans faille:
> Paie un denier ou boi encore.   (vss. 274-276)

Auberon proves difficult, however, insisting on paying the *maille* now and the *denier* when he returns later, but the Tavernkeeper, knowing he is dealing with a stranger,[9] has another trick up his sleeve. As if on cue, a second customer, Cliquet, suggests a game of dice to Auberon. The Tavernkeeper immediately tells the messenger to settle the debt with the dice: " Avés oï, sire courlieu? / Alés euwillier vostre affaire " (vss. 292-293). When Auberon wins and goes on his way, he leaves behind a disgruntled innkeeper to collect a difficult debt from the equally disgruntled dice player.

The tavern is of course the natural meeting place for thieves. Here Cliquet, whom we have seen as already in debt to the landlord, and Pincedé and Rasoir, who join him later, drink, gamble and plan

---

[8] For discussions of the wine reckonings in the *Jeu*, see: G. Frank, " Wine reckonings in Bodel's *Jeu de saint Nicolas*," *MLN*, 50 (1935), 9-13; C. E. Cousins, " Tavern Bills in the *Jeu de saint Nicolas*," *ZRP*, LVI (1936), 85-93; L. Foulet, " Les scènes de taverne dans le *Jeu de saint Nicolas*," *Rom.*, LXVIII (1944-45), 425-438; C. Foulon, " Les comptes du tavernier dans le *Jeu de saint Nicolas*," *Rom.*, LXVIII (1944-1945), 438-443. The solution proposed by Foulet and Foulon and accepted by Warne is the most satisfactory.

[9] Established in vs. 266.

their theft. The Tavernkeeper is, to say the least, tolerant of them despite their lack of money. They are customers and, on this occasion, his only source of revenue, so he allows them credit although always careful to remind them of their reckoning, never making an error to his disadvantage. He makes use of his knowledge that a thirsty customer with empty pockets will willingly promise more when drinking on credit than if the transaction is cash. Thus, when Cliquet welcomes Pincedé and orders more wine, the landlord tells Caignet to take the order but not before he has reminded Cliquet how much he owes, getting him to agree to include in the reckoning the extra *parti* he had failed to exact from Auberon:

> Cliquet, tu devoies un lot [10]
> Et puis un denier de ton gieu
> Et trois partis pour le courlieu:
> Che sont cinc deniers, poi s'en faut.  (vss. 676-679)

Cliquet's reply shows not only his willingness to pay this amount but also suggests that the practice of drinking on credit was common in Arras taverns: " Cinc denier soient, ne m'en chaut / Ainc ostes ne me trouva dur " (vss. 680-681). Another indication of this practice is to be found in *Courtois d'Arras* where prospective customers are told that credit is easy to obtain in the tavern.[11]

When the three thieves settle down to play dice to pass the time before setting out on their night's work, Cliquet requests the host for a loan. An established custom is suggested by the direct and casual approach of the borrower: " Biaus ostes, preste me une onzainne, / Si devrai dis et set par tout " (vss. 806-807).[12] The Tavernkeeper for his part showed no surprise; it seems that he regularly loaned money *au denier douze*. This supposition is borne out by Cliquet when, admitting his earlier debt, he counts:

> Che sont cinc, se je voeil encore,
> Et onze m'en presterés ore:
> Dis et set sont. Vient bien chis contes?  (vss. 815-817)

It is also confirmed by Caignet's count when Cliquet asks him how

---

[10] One *lot* costs three *deniers*; see vs. 811: " Ten premier lot che furent troi."

[11] vss. 108-113.

[12] For the earlier reading and subsequent rejection of *douzaine* for *onzainne* see Warne, p. 81, note to vs. 806.

much he owes: " Dis et set: / Cinc du vin et douze du prest " (vss. 1328-1329).

The Tavernkeeper does not allow these debts to mount up without keeping his eye on the security. The customary pledge seems to have been clothing, preferably the debtor's cloak.[13] Thus, to Rasoir's expansive invitation to drink, Cliquet demurs: " Rasoirs, nous avommes tant but / Que no drapel en demouront " (vss. 746-747), and when the Tavernkeeper grants Cliquet his loan he warns him:

> Cliquet, warde que t[u] empruntes!
> Che pues tu bien de fi savoir
> Que je vaurrai bon gage avoir;
> Tu iés mout estrains en te cape:
> J'ai paour qu'ele ne t'escape
> Ains que tu isses de l'ostel. (vss. 818-823)

Caignet bears this in mind, for when the gamblers come to blows over the dice, he calls out to his master:

> Sire, sire, vous perdés tout.
> Acourés tost, nos wage empirent!
> Car cist ribaut tout se descirent
> Et si n'ont drap qui gaires vaille! (vss. 922-925)

The Tavernkeeper's threat is ultimately carried out, for when the thieves fail in their venture and are ejected from the tavern, he orders the potboy: " Caignet, va ten escot cueillir / Puis les me met hors de mon ostel " (vss. 1322-1323), upon which Caignet turns to Cliquet with: " Or cha, Cliquet! Il n'i a el, / Delivrés vous de ceste cape! " (vss. 1324-1325)

With the prospect of a share in the loot in mind, the Tavernkeeper has no scruples in offering the thieves the shelter of his inn. Upon their return with the treasure his welcome is most warm:

> A foi, bien vegniés vous, segneur!
> Or tost, Caignet, aïe leur!
> Tes hom fait bien a rechevoir. (vss. 1022-1024)

Nothing is too good for them:

> Segneur, et biau fu et bon siege
> Arés vous, onques n'en doutés,
> Et vin qui n'est mie boutés,
> Ains crut en costiere de roche. (vss. 1030-1033)

---

[13] Cf. *Courtois d'Arras*, sc. VIII.

Although the thieves are in no hurry to share out their new-found wealth, the landlord behaves with the greatest patience and tact. When the robbers first dip into the treasure for stakes for their game of dice, he politely requests to be allowed to help himself, too: " Segneur, or doi jou apongnier? " (vs. 1070), but he defers to Cliquet's injunction to wait: " Ostes, quant au partir venra, / Bien i sera vos drois gardés " (vss. 1072-1073). He even rebukes Caignet for appearing over-anxious to take the three *deniers* promised him: " Caignet, lais les jouer en pais: / Plus atenc jou en eus de bien " (vss. 1106-1107), and with a cordial " Soiés en pais! " accepts Rasoir's assurance that he personally will safeguard the host's interests. Finally, when the game of *hasart* ends, scarcely containing his eagerness, he suggests: " Or en pregne se part chascuns . . . / Que doit que vous tant atendés? " (vss. 1180-1181) but once more he defers to Rasoir's " Ostes, un petit entendés / . . . / Bien partirommes comme ami / Mais nous arons anchois dormi " (vss. 1182, 1183-1184). When St. Nicholas dramatically intervenes, however, and orders the return of the treasure, the Tavernkeeper sees his hopes of gain vanish and exhibits a completely changed attitude. Hypocritically he refuses to take any of the wealth he has hitherto coveted, knowing full well that it is now beyond his reach, pretending not to have known that the thieves were involved in a criminal undertaking and, self-righteously disowning interest in ill-gotten gains, he orders them out of his establishment:

>Segneur, je n'en trai nient a mi
>Se vous avés fait desraison.
>Mais widiés me tost me maison,
>Car n'ai cure de tel gaaing.   (vss. 1312-1315)

When Pincedé accuses him of complicity in the theft, the last vestiges of his politeness and patience suddenly vanish and he replies in no gentle terms:

>Or hors, fil a putain, glouton!
>Volés me vous blasme acueillir?   (vss. 1320-1321)

Caignet, the potboy, complements the contribution of the Tavernkeeper to the animated realism of the Arras scenes. A faithful servant to the landlord, he is concerned chiefly with protecting his master's interests. He grumbles at the lack of profit promised by the thieves as customers of the tavern: " Par foi! Chi a povre conquest, / Car nous n'i gaaignerons waires" (vss. 684-685). If what Cliquet says is true, he gives short measure in drawing the wine: "Caignet, honnis soit or vos traires / Et qui si faussement le sache!" (vss. 686-687). He also has the reputation of being always quick to demand payment, never erring in the customer's favor; says Cliquet again: "Au conter n'iés tu point laniers / N'au mesconter, s'on te veut croire" (vss. 694-695). Cliquet's briefly expressed opinion of him is that he is "Hons qui le gent escorche et poile" (vs. 689). Besides his regular duties of drawing wine and supplying candles, for which he exacts payment with characteristic promptness, taking a *denier* from the table when the players are distracted by a quarrel (vs. 887), Caignet also provides the dice for the gamblers when Cliquet refuses to play with those of Pincedé. His greatest responsibility, however, seems to be the keeping of order among the customers, calling the Tavernkeeper when they become too quarrelsome, not, we suppose, merely for the sake of peace and quiet but to make sure that no disturbance occurs which might jeopardize the payment of the customers' debts, as in the case of the thieves' quarrel referred to above, when they threatened to tear each others' clothes. On this occasion the Tavernkeeper leaves the settling of the dispute to him and he performs the task with the force and skill of his master, whom we find intervening in two threatening arguments, the first between the criers (vss. 625-641), and the second between Pincedé and Rasoir over the outcome of the game of *hasart* (vss. 1166-1179). When the thieves' brief period of prosperity is over and they no longer appear as potential sources of profit, Caignet shows more direct powers of persuasion. His task is to collect the pledge for what is owed and to eject from the taxern the no longer desirable customers. This he does with the firmness of long practice, affecting now his master's air of respectability: "Ja n'iert sans noise ne sans frape / Hom qui si faite gent rechet" (vss. 1326-1327). He takes Cliquet's cape in payment, stifling the robber's fainthearted protests with a threat: "Encor te fai je grant bonté / Se je daigne te cape atraire" (vss. 1334-1335), drawing the last insult from the departing gambler: "De gage prendre et de mestraire / N'a ten pareil jusques au Dan!"[14] (vss. 1336-1337).

---

[14] Le Dan (Damme), former port of Bruges. See Warne, p. 90, note to vs. 1337.

It is the presence of Caignet which allows Bodel to introduce into these scenes the touch of realism afforded by the few words of thieves' jargon exchanged by Pincedé and Cliquet. The former has remarked that the wine is so good that the landlord must have made a mistake in selling it at the price they are paying (vss. 700-703). His partner exclaims:

> Santissiés pour le marc dou cois
> Et pour sen geugon qui la seme!    (vss. 704-705)

Pincedé adds:

> Voire, et qui maint bignon li teme
> Quant il trait le bai sans le marc.    (vss. 706-707)

Although the exact meaning of these lines remains obscure, despite the efforts of many critics to solve the difficulties they present, the general import is clear.[15] Cliquet seems to be telling Pincedé to hold his tongue lest the potboy who is nearby should overhear his rash remark concerning the wine. Pincedé's reply evidently is intended to cover his slip for it would seem to be a reference to some habit the potboy has of cheating his master. This is supported by Caignet's quick interruption, begging them to say no more (vss. 708-709). As Cliquet fears, the potboy evidently has caught the remark concerning the wine but Pincedé, knowing how devoted a servant he is to the Tavernkeeper, ensures that he will not take advantage of it by his cunning reference with its implied threat, slyly couched in the same jargon which Caignet must be fairly familiar with and also the landlord, judging by Caignet's concern.

Much of the action and dialogue of the scenes laid in the tavern centers around dicing. The five successive games played have been thoroughly studied by a succession of scholars.[16] and, with the explanation of the least comprehensible — the game of *hasart* — by

---

[15] For a discussion of this passage see M. Dubois, "Sur un passage obscur du *Jeu de saint Nicolas*," *Rom.*, LV (1929), 256-258, also Warne, p. 79, notes to vss. 704-705 and 706-707.

[16] R. Spitzer, *Beiträge zur Geschichte des Spiels in Alt-Frankreich* (diss. Heidelberg, 1891); F. Semrau, "Würfel und Würfelspiel im alten Frankreich," Beiheft zur *ZRP*, XXIII (1910); C. E. Cousins, "Deux parties de dés dans le *Jeu de saint Nicolas*," *Rom.*, LVII (1931), 436-437; A. Gill, "A note on the gamblers' quarrels in the *Jeu de saint Nicolas*," *Med. A.* VIII (1939), 50-53; C. A. Knudson, "Hasard et les autres jeux de dés dans le *Jeu de saint Nicolas*," *Rom.*, LXIII (1937), 248-253.

Knudson who happily thought to consult the *Libro del ajedrez, de los dados y de las tablas,* compiled for Alfonso X of Castille (1252-1284), it may be said that the difficulties seen earlier in these sections of the play have been finally cleared up. For the purposes of this study it will be sufficient to describe the games briefly, stressing here as elsewhere the contribution of the true-to-life behavior of the characters involved to the overall realism of the setting. Indeed, the very difficulties encountered in attempting to understand the exact nature and course of the games stem precisely from Bodel's interest in the players rather than in the games themselves, although, as research and careful reading have shown, the dialogue is woven around perfectly plausible dicing situations. The first game (vss. 300-309) is between Cliquet and Auberon who throw for the highest number of points (vs. 300). Cliquet scores 7 (vs. 304). Auberon does not announce his score directly—Cliquet can see it for himself—but more realistically mocks Cliquet for having to pay for what he has not tasted, i. e. Auberon's drink, and triumphantly declares: " J'ai quaernes, le plus mal gieu " (vs. 309); in other words, his two lowest dice being fours, he has won the game. The second game (vss. 852-865) is played—as are all subsequent games— by the three thieves, again for the highest score, the player on this occasion with the lowest score having to pay for the wine consumed (vss. 826-827, 843). After Pincedé's warning: " Dont giet chascuns devant le main " (vss. 850), Rasoir throws three fives. Pincedé, as Rasoir gleefully notes (vss. 856-861), scores only 5, the actual score, which the players need not be told, being given indirectly in what must be an aside of mutual congratulation directed by Rasoir, who sees his score safe, to Cliquet, who has not yet thrown (vs. 860). The chances of throwing a lower score than this are so small that Pincedé disgustedly accepts the loss of the game and excuses Cliquet from throwing: " Dehait qui te fera geter! " (vs. 862). It is before this game that Pincedé proposes that they use his dice; to Cliquet who asks: " Qui en a nul? ", Pincedé replies: " Jou, uns quarrés, / D'une vergue, drois et quemuns " (vss. 828-829).[17] Cliquet emphatically refuses the offer and Caignet's dice are used. Smarting from the defeat in this game, Pincedé immediately suggests playing for money (vs. 866), again for the highest number of

---

[17] " I have, equal-sided ones, all of a size, properly cut (*drois*: cut rectangular) and ordinary " (Warne's translation, p. 82, note to vss. 828-829).

points (vs. 874). Rasoir, apparently taking advantage of the poor light, hurriedly throws and loudly claims 12 points (vs. 880), which Cliquet quickly corrects to 10 (vs. 881), causing a slight disturbance. Again showing his fidelity to reality, Bodel has Pincedé's score indirectly and naturally conveyed to us. Pincedé, having thrown, remarks upon Rasoir's inattention (vs. 897) and Rasoir agrees that he has lost interest, for, referring to his own score, "... tu l'as passé d'un point" (vs. 898); in other words Pincedé has scored 11. Full of boasts (vss. 900-901), Cliquet throws and claims victory: "Car j'ai quaernes et un sis" (vs. 905), but Pincedé, outdone a second time, angrily protests that Cliquet's throw was unfair: "A! c'est pour nient que vous getés, / Car che fut en wanquetinois" [18] (vss. 902-903), thereby precipitating the scuffle which Caignet settles. On their return to the tavern with the treasure, the thieves play their fourth game, the person throwing the highest number of points winning the right to the first throw at *hasart*, the game suggested by Pincedé (vs. 1062). After an argument about the table being level or not (vss. 1074-1083), Rasoir throws and scores 7. Pincedé, indicating the familiarity for the fine points of the game suggested by his name, shows Rasoir the trick of rubbing the hand in the dust to allow the dice to roll freely (vss. 1088-1091) and scores 17. Dismayed by this high score, Cliquet refuses to throw and yields to Pincedé. Rasoir, equally perturbed, warns Cliquet to watch their opponent carefully: "Pour Dieu, Cliquet! Or i wardés, / Car il set les dés asseir" (vss. 1094-1095). Pincedé, then, will throw in the game of *hasart*. If his first throw is a 3, 4, 5, 6, 7, or a 14, 15, 16, 17, 18, that is *hasart*, he will win. If he throws an 8, 9, 10, 11, 12 or 13 he must throw again. If he throws *hasart* on this second throw, he loses; but if he gets another number, then he continues throwing until he repeats the first number, in which case he loses, or the second number, when he wins, the first of these being his opponents' "chance" and the second his "chance" as thrower. With passionately expressed wishes from all three players Pincedé throws and scores 13, the "chance" of Cliquet and Rasoir. Despite Rasoir's vociferous wish for the second throw to be *hasart* (vs. 1115), dropped dice (vs. 1117), Cliquet's advice as to how to throw (vss. 1118-1119, 1122), Pincedé throws 8, his "chance" which he must repeat to win: "Or laissiés treize a uit

---

[18] Wanquetin is a village seven miles west of Arras.

combatre" (vs. 1128). Now follows an undetermined number of throws, causing tense excitement (vss. 1132-1139), culminating in Pincedé's triumphant cry: "Vés chi uit, che sont mi ami" (vs. 1139). The modern reader will readily appreciate the humorous realism of these games, *hasart* in particular being instantly recognizable as the ancestor of dice games universally played today, while the behavior, comments, exclamations, accusations and indignant protests of these gamblers of the twelfth century are no whit outdated.

Comment on the wine in the tavern scenes plays an important part in heightening their familiar coloring and in reinforcing the realism of the dialogue and setting. The wine sold by the Tavernkeeper is that of Auxerre, well known in the Middle Ages;[19] In the *Desputoison du vin et de l'iaue*,[20] speaking for the wines of Burgundy, the wine of Auxerre says: "Sire, je sui .1. Aucuerrois/ Qui sus tous vins doi estre rois" (p. 295). From the remarks of the Tavernkeeper and of his customers, this wine—at least the wine served in the tavern under the same name—would appear to be strong, full-bodied and thick; the lower in the barrel the better it tastes:[21] "Un vin qui point ne file" (vs. 257); "Tien, chis te montera ou chief; / Boi bien, li mieudres est au fons" (vss. 268-269); "Caignet, abaisse un poi le broche, / Si nous laisse taster au tourble" (vss. 1034-1035); ". . . et vin / Mieudres que il ne fu deseure" (vss. 1040-1041). Such comments as these and the many exchanges like that between the thieves upon their return to the inn from their apparently successful venture, when their single thought is to make the most of their wealth and drink deep and long, present a picture of low-life characters always thirsting for wine and far more concerned with its quantity and strength than with its finer qualities. In strong contrast is the idealized description of the wine as the vendor would have the public think of it, given by the professional crier, Raoulet:

[19] For a list of references in medieval works to this wine, see *Cortebarbe*, index, p. 17, under *Aucoirre*.

[20] *Nouveau recueil de contes, dits, fabliaux et autres pièces inédites des XIIIe, XIVe et XVe siècles*, ed. Achille Jubinal (Paris, 1839), I, 293-311.

[21] It need hardly be said that this criterion reflects not the quality of the wine but the Tavernkeeper's greed for profit and the patrons' desire to drink as much as possible.

> Le vin aforé de nouvel,
> A plain lot et a plain tonnel,
> Sade, bevant, et plain et gros,
> Rampant comme escuireus en bos,
> Sans nul mors de pourri ne d'aigre;
> Seur lie court et sec et maigre,
> Cler con larme de pecheour,
> Croupant seur langue a lecheour;
> Autre gent n'en doivent gouster.    (vss. 645-652)
>
> Vois con il mengüe s'escume
> Et saut et estinchele et frit!
> Tien le seur le langue un petit,
> Si sentiras ja outrevin.    (vss. 658-661)

In the same vein is the phrase used by the Tavernkeeper when he wishes to impress his newly rich customers:

> Et vin qui n'est mie boutés,
> Ains crut en costiere de roche.    (vss. 1032-1033)

In these phrases is to be seen another reflection of medieval city life, another allusion likely to awaken broad associations in the mind of the audience, another detail giving solidity to the realistic background of the miracle: medieval advertising. For us, as it did for Bodel's audience, Raoulet's speech immediately assumes this familiar shape with its extravagant claims of quality, its piled-up qualifications of excellence, its lyrical similes and metaphors, its " snob appeal " (vss. 651-652), its final tempting visual description and the ultimate invitation to taste the product. To the Arras audience, moerover, the very terms and images of the speech were familiar, for Bodel utilized those in general use, as is shown by comparison with many medieval texts concerned with the praise of wine. Thus, in the *Desputoison,* the wine of Auxerre says:

> Mes je sui eler saillant en voire,
> Fins, fres, froit, sade, fremiant,
> Sasfres, savoureus et friant.    (Jubinal, pp. 297-298)

In *Courtois d'Arras,* Lequet, speaking of the wine he is serving, says: " Voies com fait le lionchel. / Il est d'auchoirre (vss. 206-207), to which Pourette replies: " Tenes, com sade et bien bevant / le poes maintenant sentir " (vss. 210-211). Other examples of similar descriptions of wine have been noted by Clédat [22] and by

---

[22] " Sur un dicton auxerrois du XIIIe siècle," *RLR,* XXII (1882), 99-101.

Meyer.[23] The latter, in discussing the phenomenon of alliteration in the lauding of wine, brings to our attention an Anglo-Norman *dit* preserved in two fourteenth century manuscripts.[24] These list the qualities to be sought in a good wine and among the adjectives applicable appear many of those used by Raoulet.[25] Even stronger evidence of the existence of the general fund of stock expressions upon which Bodel drew is to be seen in the following phrases taken from the same manuscripts: " Il crust sur le croupel de la mountaigne . . . estencele cum carbon de chenvert, rampaunt cum esquirel du boys . . . cler cum lerme de senge qe plort par force de vent." (Lansdowne). " Ceo vin crut en croupe de mountaygne . . . raumpaunt come esquirel . . . il set [su]r lange de leccher " (Old Royal).

The crying of the wine and of the king's proclamations concerning first the mobilization of his subjects to meet the Christian invasion and later the deliberate exposure of the royal treasure introduces another medieval personage, the town crier. Bodel's use of this figure is, however, another particular reflection of the Arras scene. He introduces two criers. The first, Connart, describes himself thus:

> Amis, on m'apele Connart;
> Crïeres sui par naïté
> As eskievins de la chité.
> Soisante ans a passés, et plus,
> Que de crïer me sui vescus. (vss. 602-606)

The second, Raoulet, says of himself:

> J'ai non Raouls qui le vin cri,
> Si sui as homes de le vile. (vss. 608-609)

---

[23] " De l'allitération en roman de France, à propos d'une formule allitérée relative aux qualités du vin," *Rom*, XI (1882), 572-579.

[24] British Museum. MS. Old Royal, 12 D. XI, last folio, recto, printed by Wright and Halliwell, *Reliquiae antiquae*, I, 273-274, and MS. Lansdowne 397, folio 9, verso, printed II, 29, both reprinted by Meyer in the article cited above.

[25] *bon, bel, blanc, court, cresp, cler, sein, sad, saverouse, net, nais, natureus, fin, fres, froit, fort, frick, flurant, freignant, furmente* (Old Royal); *bons, beus, bevale, court, clers, crespe, net, neays, naturels, sek, sayn, sade, freit, fresche, friant, fremissant, furmentel, feire, fyn, fraunceys* (Lansdowne).

Herein lies a direct reference to the administration of Arras. In 1194 Arras was granted, by royal charter, an autonomous magistrature, composed of twelve officials with full powers of jurisdiction, and twelve purely administrative functionaries, *échevins de la cité* and *hommes de la ville* respectively.[26] It is highly probable that between the criers of these two official bodies disputes were not unusual. Moreover, in view of the undoubted importance of the crying of wine in medieval cities [27] and the brief and otherwise scarcely significant self-portrait of Connart, it would not be unreasonable to suppose that the subject and characters of the incident in the play are founded on fact.

The action and the characterization of the tavern scenes leave no doubt that they are Arrasian, but if further evidence were needed it could be found in the few references in the text to places near Arras. To Bodel's audience, however, no such evidence was necessary, so the value of these references must be sought elsewhere. It would seem to lie, in fact, in the effect writers of comic scenes universally derive from introducing into situations and dialogue names familiar to the audience, with humorous intent, the use of the particular name in a particular situation causing amusement by strikingly apt or inapt association. Underlying the use of the name is a common knowledge of particular characteristics of the place. We no longer have this knowledge of the places mentioned in the *Jeu*, but it is entirely reasonable to suppose that their introduction into the play provided this " local humor." It is in this light that we must understand Pincedé's accusation that Cliquet cheated in throwing the dice " Car che fu en wanquetinois " (vs. 903). Similarly, the same character's exclamation following Raoulet's praise of the wine might have caused amusement by the very appositeness of his metaphor involving another village near Arras: " Hé Diex! c'est chi blés de Henin! " [28] (vs. 662). Finally, it is not to be

---

[26] Guesnon, *op. cit.*, p. 73, note 2.

[27] The division of the criers' duties into the King's and the magistrates' business on the one hand and, on the other, the crying of the wine, indicated in the *Jeu* both by the criers' opening remarks and the Tavernkeeper's decision settling their dispute, suggests that the crier of wine, with tankard and stick as emblems of his office (vss. 612-616), was a person of some responsibility.

[28] Warne (index, p. 112), identifies Henin with Hénin-Liétard near Lens, about 15 miles N. E. of Arras, famous for its wheat. The humor of these

doubted that Cliquet's plan for his next nefarious undertaking is in the same vein of humor. He says he is off to " Fraisne / Un petit dela Gaverele " (vss. 1370-1371) where he will work mischief on the mayor. Pincedé's warning: " Cliquet, li mairesse est mout sage / Si te connistra au passer " (vss. 1374-1375) seems to add to the point of a joke depending on some peculiar circumstance of the village named which must have been familiar to Bodel's listeners if not to us.

Although taking no part in the action of the tavern scenes, the jailer is yet another character who belongs to the medieval city. Armed with a *machue* and *tenailles*, with which he threatens to pull out the teeth of the Preudom, and with his talk of a slow death for his victim (vss. 1227-1228) and of hanging him by the thumbs and again of pulling out his teeth (vss. 1413-1414), he must have represented to the Arras audience, if not particular Arras individual—he is described only in the most general of terms—then at least a familiar type, calling to mind the jailer and hangman of their own city.

The tavern scenes of the *Jeu de saint Nicolas* vividly recreate, then, a realistic Arras atmosphere. Place, characters, and customs on the one hand and the lifelike behavior and dialogue on the other, containing countless local allusions and flashes of popular humor, undoubtedly impressed the audiences with their familiarity and realistic proportion, the grotesque and the fantastic being conspicuously absent. It now remains to be seen how Bodel integrated the action of the story developed in the crusading scenes with the action of the story in the tavern scenes. Taken separately, these stories might well have an independent existence but they are blended together naturally and logically in such a way as to cause the *Iconia* legend of St. Nicholas, of secondary importance in each of the separate stories, to emerge as the real subject of the drama, justifying our acceptance of it as a miracle play.

---

words of Pincedé would come not from a spirit of satire but from the somewhat pathetic association of a familiar little village, proud of its homely produce, with the ecstatic, lyrical world of sensual delight, conjured up by Raoulet's encomium of the widely renowned wine of Auxerre.

## CHAPTER V

### INTEGRATION

The clear influence of the crusading zeal of its day upon it notwithstanding, the *Jeu de saint Nicolas* is not, as Le Roy and Lintilhac would have it, " de la tragédie nationale," essentially inspired by the momentous events of the crusades of the thirteenth century under the leadership of France. Neither, despite the extensive use of epic material, is it a dramatized *chanson de geste*. These views do not take into account the presence and extent of the popular scenes. On the other hand, the *Jeu* is not, as Petit de Julleville considered it, merely a popular tale of roguery in a realistic tavern setting, a dramatized *fabliau* as it were, the rough tone of which is alleviated by a few moving scenes of patriotic appeal. To subscribe to either of these main points of view is to ignore the significance of the aspect of the play stressed by the other. Both, moreover, entail a neglect of the hagiographic element and lead to the consideration of the saint's legend as nothing more than an excuse to present other matters. It is scarcely more satisfactory to adopt Rohnstroem's compromise. Although free of the earlier bias in favor of one or other of the main features of the *Jeu* and recognizing the saint's legend as its motif, he is content to dwell separately on these various aspects and seeks no unity of conception or construction which would embrace them. Bodel must be held in higher esteem. If Petit de Julleville writes disparagingly of the *Jeu*, attributing its qualities and appeal to the capricious invention of the childish mind of the thirteenth century—" dans l'ordre littéraire au moins, l'âme de ce siècle était plus voisin de l'enfance qu'est la nôtre " [1]—then Bodel is ably defended as a poet with a sense of vocation and mature imagination by Gaston Paris. Paying tribute to Bodel's preeminence as a playwright and referring to his merit in other genres of literary expression, he praises him as " ce poëte qui, dès la fin du douzième siècle, avait fait un effort au moins remarquable pour renouveler et soumettre à un art plus raffiné la forme épique; qui avait donné à la poésie lyrique un caractère de personnalité presque poignant; et qui en même temps,

---

[1] Petit de Julleville, *Mystères*, I, 107.

par son œuvre, singulière mais puissante, du *Jeu de saint Nicolas*, avait du premier coup indiqué la voie où pouvait marcher une dramaturgie nationale." [2] The power that Gaston Paris sensed in the *Jeu* springs from its essential unity. It is not sufficient to explain the play in terms of its component elements alone, although, when examined separately, they are seen to be of great merit. Of transcendent worth is their skillful integration in subject and in form, the fusion of their separate identities in a unified recreation of the *Iconia* legend, in a miracle play, the dramatic expression of a poetic conception of the place of a great and familiar saint in the lives of people of Arras in the twelfth century.

Despite the characteristic epic material of which it is composed and which gives it the appearance of a miniature *chanson de geste*, the crusading story in the *Jeu* differs in one major respect from the Old French epics. Generally, the epics of the Charlemagne and of the William of Orange cycles have as their mainspring the threefold loyalty to God, to the Emperor or Count, and to the tradition of heroic knighthood. The epic scenes of the *Jeu* clearly illustrate loyalty to God and to the traditions of knighthood, but of political allegiance to a temporal ruler or military leader there is no mention. The Christian forces are always described as such, and on no occasion is a leader referred to either by name or rank. Compensation is found in the extra emphasis upon loyalty to God, direct or through the service and worship of St. Nicholas. In a sense St. Nicholas replaces Charlemagne and William, for the revenge for the Christian defeat and the rescue of the captured Preudom from the Saracen jail, typical of epic situations which usually the Emperor or Count resolve by their intervention, are here accomplished by the intervention of the saint. In our earlier analysis of the epic content of the *Jeu* little attention was paid to the rôle of the saint, the object being to estimate the extent of Bodel's debt to the *chansons de geste*. In reality the testing of the powers of the saint is the kernel of the action. The saving of the Preudom and the fulfillment of the Christian mission in the conversion of the Saracen country, the double outcome of the story, depend entirely upon it while the events leading up to the capture of the Preudom and his claim in respect of the powers of the saint are, from the point of view of the intrigue, only preparatory. In

---

[2] Gaston Paris, *Histoire poétique*, p. 110.

fact, although so much of the material of the story is epic commonplace, the excision of the theme of loyalty to a suzerain and the additional emphasis on devotion to God and his saint transform it into a hagiographical work in which the epic element is subordinate. Although the characters of the drama are almost all Saracen or low-life (as ostensible subjects of the King of Africa these are Saracen too) St. Nicholas, the Preudom, and the Angel counterbalance them all. Far from the legend of St. Nicholas being the excuse for a crusading story, it is the crusading story which serves as a vehicle for the legend.

The much simpler action of the tavern scenes, also, depends on the intervention of the saint for its outcome. If we turn to the crusading story for the development of the main intrigue, in the tavern scenes we must recognize the recreation of Arras and the all-important background for the miracle. In conformity with his object of portraying St. Nicholas as his fellow citizens of Arras conceived of him, it is in the realistic atmosphere of the tavern and to the thieves that Bodel has the saint appear, not to the Preudom or to the Saracen King in Africa. Hence the detailed and generously depicted setting of the tavern scenes fulfills its purpose only upon the appearance of the saint and, therefore, like the crusading scenes, must be seen as part of the preparation for the accomplishment of the miracle. Here, too, it is evident that the *Iconia* legend is not the excuse for scenes of popular realism but that these scenes serve as a vehicle for the representation of the legend.

The common focus of the plot that is developed chiefly in the crusading scenes and of the setting of the tavern scenes with their own essential but less developed contribution to the action, is the miraculous intervention of St. Nicholas. That this same event is the focus of the many distinct facets of the play it is possible to discern by considering the interests of individual characters separately. The King, the Emirs, the Tavernkeeper, and the thieves, are all profoundly affected by the miraculous event but each in a particular way. But to isolate these facets of the story and to distinguish sharply between the intrigue of the crusade and the atmosphere of Arras, while admitting the common focus of the miracle is not to appreciate Bodel's skill to the full. The story of the *Iconia* legend as Bodel presents it is a well-integrated complex of all such distinguishable facets whose characters, incidents, and places coincide and overlap to form a series of links between the crusading scenes and the Arras setting, constantly drawing these dissimilar elements together, indicating the common climax and underlining the essential unity of the drama.

Before seeking to illustrate Bodel's skillful integration of these dissimilar elements, we must first consider the place of the Arras settings in the dramatization of an event which presumably takes place in a Saracen land. All we know of this Saracen land is that it is a possession of the King of Africa and borders upon a Christian country. It is not named and no topographical features are described. This lack of identification leads us to believe that, to Bodel, the place of the accomplishment of the miracle is of no interest. His attention is fixed upon the miracle itself. Since this involves the protection of the treasure whose owner, as a result, embraces Christianity, and the saving of a distressed Christian, the setting is necessarily a heathen—ergo Saracen—land. The *Jeu*, however, was written for the edification and amusement of an Arras twelfth century audience, the subject of the play being St. Nicholas, a popular and highly regarded saint, very familiar to the common man and an integral part of his daily life. Hence, in view of the audience and the subject of the play, its idiom and background were inevitably, it would seem, realistic, familiar, Arrasian. If the *Jeu* were merely the dramatization of the *Iconia* legend, the setting would be Saracen and the Arras atmosphere would obtrude. Since it is a miracle play, an edifying expression of the devotion of the medieval man to his saint, written for an Arras audience, the Saracen setting fades and the Arrasian colors become significant. While from a strictly logical point of view the existence of an Arras atmosphere so strong as to be a setting for an action taking place in some Saracen land presents an incongruity, from the esthetic point of view there is no incongruity since the disparate elements are reconciled in the underlying unity of the play. We may now proceed to the illustration of Bodel's integration of the dissimilar elements of the *Jeu* and see how, in developing his story of the *Iconia* legend, he shapes it with his fertile but controlled imagination to serve the essential unity of the drama.

The Saracen King, with his seneschal and Emirs, belongs to an exotic background and his story might well be considered, in isolation, as a fantasy of the world of the characters of the *chansons de geste*. Yet in the King's employ is Connart, the crier, who proclaims the royal *bans*, ostensibly to an African crowd, but who, as is shown by his quarrel with Raoulet, crying the wine for the Arras Tavernkeeper, also occupies a natural rôle as a medieval city crier. Auberon, although a Saracen, is equally at home in the tavern where he naturally pauses for refreshment while on his mission to summon the assistance of the King's vassals. Stranger though he may be to the Tavernkeeper, he is nevertheless familiar enough with tavern life to be able to outwit the wily Tavernkeeper and the dice-player, Cliquet. He is, then, a major factor in the integration of plot and setting. Also in the service of the King is Durant, the jailer, who, although taking no part in the action centering around the tavern, is clearly a character typical of the Arras scene. The closest link between Africa and Arras, involving an essential part of the action of the legend, is provided by Cliquet, Pincedé, and Rasoir. Obviously medieval and perhaps copies of Arras characters and the central figures in the establishing of the local setting, they are the ones who steal and replace the treasure of the King of Africa, Rasoir having heard the *ban* concerning it before joining his companions in crime in the tavern. It is to them alone, as we have already noted, that St. Nicholas appears. At the sorry conclusion of their abortive attempt to make their fortune, having unwittingly played a vital part in the vindication of the Preudom's claim concerning the powers of the saint, they slip back into the Arras shadows.

The effectiveness of Bodel's account of the *Iconia* legend of St. Nicholas derives largely from its dramatic form and from its construction. The immediacy of the impact of a visual representation and the scope for spectacle and action afforded by the medieval stage was well suited to the subject. The structure of the play is characterized by a natural sequence of events and skillful introduction of characters and a careful preparation throughout for changes in scene and the eventual outcome. It is a well knit drama, logically developed from exposition through crisis to the dénouement, and which, as it directs its events towards their climax, successfully weds them to the special setting. The King is told of the invasion of his domain by a Christian army. The presence of the idol, Tervagant, serves effectively to exhibit his violence and outraged pride and the more diplomatic attitude of his seneschal. The device of the oracular pronouncement made by the idol gives the audience a glimpse of the forthcoming ebb and flow of the action and of the ultimate success of the Christian cause, as he indicates with signs that the King will at first enjoy success but eventually suffer defeat. This high note of Saracen crisis which opens the play calls for action in the shape of mobilization, so Connart is charged with the duty of crying the King's call to arms (Sc. I). Connart, in his aspect of medieval crier, and already distinguished by his name as a representative of low-life, gives the first hint of the development of the Arras atmosphere, although ostensibly he addresses the exotic peoples of the Saracen country (Sc. II). As a part of the same mobilization move the King sends Auberon to summon his great vassals from their distant territories (Sc. III). On his journey Auberon stops at the tavern, immediately recognizable as typical of Arras, and the first true indication of the background for the miracle to come. The Tavernkeeper is naturally present at the tavern and Cliquet, the first of the thieves, who will be instrumental in the accomplishment of the miracle, is neatly brought into the stream of the action by the well contrived game of dice which settles Auberon's dispute with the host (Sc. IV). Auberon completes his journey and in delivering the royal summons to the four Emirs gives them the opportunity to reveal something of their own characters and further to enhance the power of the King as a great Saracen emperor (Sc. V). This characterization is further developed when the Emirs arrive at the court of the King with their armies and rich gifts, closely following Auberon's return (Scs. VI and VII). The assembled Saracen forces are ordered into battle (Sc. VIII). A sudden change of scene to the camp of the Christian army, waiting for the attack of the enemy, creates the impression of an impending clash, while the appearance of the angel with words of comfort giving promise of a disastrous conflict serves to heighten the suspense (Sc. IX). The last violent boasts of the Emirs take us to the brink of the engagement (Sc. X). Here appears in the text the simple rubric: "Or tuent li sarrasin tous les crestïens." This bare phrase is the indication of what was probably one of the most spectacular episodes on the stage Bodel was writing for and must be accorded full value. The battle over, the story would seem to be at an end, but the audience has many questions in mind arising from the oracular message of Tervagant and from the careful introduction of the tavern scene, both of which have implications reaching far beyond the otherwise conclusive nature of the battle. Knowing the outcome of the story in general terms, the onlookers are left in a state of eager anticipation as to the way in which it is to be achieved. The key is provided in the conclusion of the scene which shows the all-important discovery of the Preudom praying to his "mahommet cornu." [3] The angel, who, in keeping with tradition, previously appeared to the Christians, now plausibly reappears to view the fallen knights and to reassure us that their souls are now with God and he is able to answer the Preudom's prayer to St. Nicholas —now mentioned for the first time—to save him from the tyrants. The answer is oracular, the angel's promise that the Christian will, if his faith in God and the saint is steadfast, have God's "haut confort," leaving us to wonder whether the Preudom will share the martyrdom of the crusaders or whether he will, in this world, be saved from the clutches of the Saracens (Sc. XI). Dragged before the King and questioned about his "mahommet cornu" the Preudom naturally fully describes the miraculous powers of the saint, adding almost as an afterthought, by way of stressing his ability to protect whatever is entrusted to him, that he could even safely guard this palace if it were full of gold. This apparent afterthought is the mainspring of the action which now moves swiftly forward again, for the King is so impressed by this material aspect of the saint's power that he immediately puts it to the test, throwing the Preudom into jail meanwhile (Sc. XII). A brief glimpse of Durant taking charge of the prisoner emphasizes the latter's desperate plight (Sc. XIII). Now, with the Christian forces destroyed and the Preudom held as guarantor for the miraculous power he has perhaps rashly claimed for his saint, the fortunes of the Christians are at a low ebb, which necessitates the second appearance of the angel to the Preudom with the promise of St. Nicholas' help. The King and his vassals, moreover, will, we are now told, be converted to Christianity (Sc. XIV). With the Preudom securely held, the King has Connart announce the exposure of his treasure, thus setting in motion the machinery for the testing of St. Nicholas (Scs. XV and XVI). This second appearance of Connart transfers the scene to the tavern again, through his realistic quarrel with the other crier, Raoulet, who happens to be crying the wine for the Tavernkeeper (Sc. XVII). Raoulet's crying

---

[3] Foulon, in *Mélanges Cohen*, p. 63, shows an awareness of the importance of the figure of the Preudom to the drama.

introduces the second of the three thieves, Pincedé, who attracted by the praise of the wine, enters the tavern to quench his thirst (Sc. XVIII). There he meets his old friend, Cliquet, and shortly they are joined by the third man of the trio, Rasoir, who brings news of the *ban* he has just heard from Connart. The full emphasis is now on the low-life setting, strongly Arrasian in every detail of action and dialogue and countless allusion. For the very good reason of having to wait for the darkest part of the night before availing themselves of the opportunity offered by the King's proclamation, they remain in the tavern, whiling away the time in drinking and dicing. Bodel is thus able to paint the scene in elaborate detail and to bring the atmosphere to the heights of realism so that there shall be no doubt as to the milieu in which St. Nicholas shall appear (Sc. XX). This shift of emphasis is shown also by the scene of the actual theft, so simply portrayed as to be little more than a brief interlude in the tavern scene (Sc. XXI). The rogues return to the inn to spend the rest of the night, as they began it, with wine and dice and much quarrelsome talk (Sc. XXII). We return to the palace of the King and his discovery of the theft (Sc. XXIII). The Preudom is dragged from the jail to answer for the failure of the saint to protect the royal treasure (Sc. XXIV). The fortunes of the Christians are now at their lowest ebb, since St. Nicholas has apparently utterly failed them. The King tells the Preudom that his God obviously has deserted him and condemns him to death. The Preudom makes his last plea for respite and the King grants it (Sc. XXV). Back in jail the wretched Christian, steadfast in his faith, prays once more to St. Nicholas, his hope still, but his last one (Sc. XXVI). The angel appears to him again and promises him the saint's immediate help (Sc. XXVII). We left the thieves sleeping in the tavern after their night's work, exhausted by the drinking and their stormy games of dice. It is here that the next scene takes place, the culmination of the intrigue, the sudden release of the tension portrayed in the situation of the Preudom and the single act which solves all the problems which have kept the audience in suspense. With what technical stage effects we can only surmise, St. Nicholas himself makes a dramatic appearance, rousing the thieves and throwing them into a state of terror with his threats of death unless they immediately restore the treasure exactly as they found it (Scs. XXVIII and XXIX). The solution is now clear and the play moves swiftly to its end, not without full respect for the characterization. The Tavernkeeper, fearful of the consequences of his part in the thieves' robbery, hastily ejects them from his establishment (Sc. XXX). The thieves replace the treasure and sink back into the city shadows (Sc. XXXI). The King discovers the treasure back in place and hails a miracle (Sc. XXXII). The final scene brings the release of the Preudom, his prayers for his deliverance answered, his claim as to the powers of the saint vindicated, and the conversion of the Saracens as promised by the angel.

There can be no doubt as to Bodel's skill as a playwright. In casting his story in dramatic form he bore the audience constantly in mind, and sought to convey with clarity, plausibility and economy, succeeding events, changes of scene, and the introduction and direction of the characters. He made excellent use of the multiple stage, avoiding confusing excess of movement and dispersal of scenes, yet adequately representing the necessary movement without detracting from the proportions in the overall setting demanded by the subject. The opening scenes in the King's palace, the assembly of the vessels, the battle, the climactic appearance of St. Nicholas, and the closing scene portraying the renunciation of the heathen faith, give ample scope for lively action and vivid spectacle and, by contrast, make the popular scenes which constitute the main body of the play equally impressive.

## CHAPTER VI

### VERSIFICATION

The versification of the *Jeu* in itself belies the opinion that Bodel's work is the product of a precocious and unsophisticated imagination. A close examination shows an intelligent use of rhyme and meter, constantly heightening the effect of the varying tone and reinforcing the structure of this miracle play. The Prologue is composed of octosyllabic rhyming couplets, the normal form for narrative verse at this time, imparting a swiftness of movement to phrases and sentences of normal length and construction and ensuring here a clear well-paced introduction to the play. In the Prologue, as throughout the *Jeu*, a high standard of rhyming is observed, rhymes being not only frequently rich (*victoire: estoire*, vss. 27-28; *veille: merveille*, vss. 105-106; *pierre: espiere*, vss. 783-784, etc.), but even leonine (*garder: larder*, vss. 39-40; *desmané: engané*, vss. 63-64; *travillier: awillier*, vss. 287-288; *ourant: plourant*, vss. 511-512, etc.). Faulty rhymes (*Arbre: Arabe*, vss. 333-334; *pec: mer*, vss. 367-368; *serviche: brise*, vss. 402-403; *chiers: aprés*, vss. 492-493, etc.) are few.[1] The tavern scenes also, with one exceptional passage, are entirely in octosyllabic rhymed couplets, the most suitable form for popular dialogue where swift repartee and an abundance of short phrases, the normal exchange of colloquial conversation, require a natural line and the simplest of rhyme schemes. The crusading scenes exhibit a considerable variety of meter and rhyme.[2] The general line is octosyllabic, disposed in sextets rhymed a a b c c b,[3] the slightly more elevated action gain-

---

[1] For a detailed examination of Bodel's rhyme, see Warne, p. xxviii.

[2] The more complex versification of the crusading scenes is as follows (except where otherwise indicated, the verse form is the octosyllabic sextet rhyming a a b c c b):

* Sc. I, vss. 115-170. King told of invasion—*octosyllabic couplets*.
  171-224. Oracle and order to call out the army.
  III, vss. 239-250. King sends Auberon on mission—*alexandrine monorhymed quatrains*.
  V, vss. 315-338. Auberon delivers summons to Emirs.
  VI, vss. 339-348. Auberon reports back to King—*octosyllabic couplets*.
  VII, vss. 349-383. Arrival of Emirs (for irregularity of vss. 373-377 see note 3 below).

ing in sobriety and sophistication from the more complex rhyme scheme. Interspersed are scenes written in alexandrine monorhymed quatrains, reflecting the epic atmosphere of the passages involving the Saracen and Christian conflict: the King sending his summons to the great vassals of his vast empire (Sc. III), the King ordering his assembled forces into battle (Sc. VIII), the Christians nobly anticipating the fierce onslaught of the enemy and addressing solemn words to the Angel sent to comfort them (Sc. IX, vss. 396-411, 424-427).

The rhyme scheme and meter, however, cannot be regarded as

VIII, vss. 384-395. King sends army into battle—*alexandrine monorhymed quatrains.*

IX, vss. 396-411, 424-427. Christian knights see enemy and speak to Angel—*alexandrine monorhymed quatrains.*

IX, vss. 412-423, 428-435. Angel speaks to knights—*octosyllabic couplets.*

X, vss. 436-465. Emirs attack, route Christians and capture Preudom.

XI, vss. 466-481. Angel to fallen knights—*2 octosyllabic stanzas a b a b c c d d.*

XI, vss. 482-487. Preudom prays.

XI, vss. 488-495. Angel comforts Preudom—*octosyllabic couplets.*

XII, XIII, vss. 496-549. Preudom brought before King and jailed.

XIV, vss. 550-560. Angel comforts Preudom—*alexandrine couplet a a, 7 six-syllable lines a a b b b c c, 2 octosyllabic unrhymed lines?* (See note 4 below.)

XV, vss. 561-578. King orders treasure entrusted to image.

XXIII-XXVI, vss. 1187-1264. King discovers loss of treasure, condemns Preudom to death, reprieves him. Preudom prays to St. Nicholas.

XXVII, vss. 1265-1278. Angel encourages Preudom—*decasyllabic monorhymed quatrains.*

XXXII, vss. 1383-1406. King discovers treasure restored.

XXXIII, vss. 1407-1472. King frees Preudom and with Seneschal is converted.

1473-1538. Emirs' conversion and destruction of Tervagant—*octosyllabic couplets.*

[3] Sc. I, vss. 171-224 clearly follows this pattern. Warne (p. xvii) holds that vss. 173-224 are sextets of a different rhyme pattern—a b b a c c— the scene ending in an irregular stanza x y y z. Sc. VII, vss. 373-377, rhyming a a b b c is evidently a corruption of the original stanza which could be read as a a [b?] c c b, assuming a line missing between vss. 374 and 375. Warne (p. xvii) sees vs. 377 as an orphan line and would complete the stanza by taking the first couplet of the next—vss. 378-379—the remainder of the stanza becoming an irregular form—a quatrain a b b a.

solely an attempt to emphasize the tone of particular scenes. Exceptions exist to the tendency noted above in respect of the crusading and tavern scenes; in the former, couplets are found and in the latter, sextets. Also the use of four different meters to convey the angel's messages makes it necessary to seek other functions for the versification. The four different meters used for the words of the angel are: octosyllabic rhymed couplets in the address to the knights before the battle (Sc. IX, vss. 412-423, 428-435); an octosyllabic series rhymed a b a b c c d d, repeated in the address to the fallen knights (Sc. XI, vss. 466-481); octosyllabic couplets as before, in the first speech to the Preudom (Sc. XI, vss. 488-495); a series of two rhymed alexandrines, seven lines of six syllables rhyming a a b b b c c, and two octosyllabic lines unrhymed, in the second message to the Preudom (Sc. XIV, vss. 550-560)[4] and, finally, decasyllabic quatrains in monorhyme in the last words of comfort to the Preudom (Sc. XXVII, vss. 1265-1278).[5] These apparent aberrations do not justify the opinion that any coincidence between the versification and the action is fortuitous. They can be explained as an attempt by Bodel to employ contrast, through changes in versification, to emphasize or indicate changes in scene and, in the case of the angel, to set his words, divine in origin, apart from the dialogue of the human characters. Thus the angel's first speech, though in octosyllabic rhymed couplets, is set between alexandrine quatrains; his second speech in the same scene, also in octosyllabic couplets, follows an alexandrine quatrain and is followed by the first octosyllabic sextet of the next scene. The first speech of his second appearance, the sixteen lines of octosyllabic lines, is set between regular sextets, as is also the second speech, a series of four octosyllabic rhymed couplets. The third appearance is marked by a similar change, the complex stanza of alexandrines, six syllable and eight syllable lines also coming between regular sextets. The final appearance of the angel

[4] This arrangement of vss. 550-560 is Warne's reading of an uncertain passage in the MS. Instead of a strophe of 11 lines—alexandrines, six and eight syllable lines—Jeanroy makes an arrangement of 14 six syllable lines, the thirteenth missing and the fourteenth incomplete, the rhyme scheme being a b a b c c d d d e e f [f?] g g. Warne justifies his arrangement, p. 77, note to vss. 559-560.

[5] Vss. 1269-1270—an alexandrine followed by an octosyllabic line rhyming with it—appear to be a refrain, a later addition destroying the symmetry of the three decasyllabic stanzas, and are so considered by Rohnstroem, p. 70, and Jeanroy in the *Notes critiques* to his edition.

is marked by decasyllabic quatrains again between octosyllabic sextets.

The beginning of each low-life scene introduces a change of the verse form to octosyllabic rhymed couplets. By "scene" is meant, not the modern division based on the entrance and exit of characters found in the editions of Warne and Jeanroy, but the phase of the action taking place in one location. Thus vss. 597-994, for example, dealing with consecutive events in the region of the tavern, are taken as a scene, no change of location being involved; the same passage in Warne's edition is divided into five scenes. In this particular scene as, indeed, in others, the verse form is consistently octosyllabic couplets in rhyme. The sole exception to this is the scene embracing vss. 995-1024, describing the actual theft of the treasure. These lines are in octosyllabic sextets. The reason we may assume is Bodel's intention to highlight this incident and set it in relief against the long sequence of couplets of the preceding and following tavern scenes.

The crusading scenes follow the same principles of versification. The opportunity for special meters and rhyme schemes afforded by the battle scenes and the appearances of the angel, introduces the possibility of a great variety of change. Again ignoring the modern system of scenic division, an examination of the complex succession of scenes of this aspect of the *Jeu* shows again that a change of scene coincides with a change in versification. Thus it is that vss. 399-348, dealing with Auberon reporting to the King the successful accomplishment of his mission are, unexpectedly in the crusading context, in octosyllabic rhymed couplets. Evidently for the sake of clarity, Bodel found it effective to contrast this scene with the preceding one in which Auberon speaks to the Emirs in their several countries and with the following one in which the Emirs arrive before the King. A special use of octosyllabic couplets is to be noted in the opening and closing scenes of the play (vss. 115-170 and 1473-1538). The change to, in the one case, and in the other from the regular sextet, is clearly intentional. In the first scene the King has been informed of the Christian invasion, has abused Tervagant and, on the Seneschal's advice, has approached the idol in an attitude of penitence, "a nus genous et a nus keutes." He addresses the idol in couplets as he does this, but when he begins his prayer, "Sire, li tiens secours me viegne . . ." (vs. 171), the form changes to sextets. This precise point marks the beginning of the action after the exposition. What the exact effect is on the ear of such a change in the versification is not easy to determine; in all probability it creates the impression of a moving into high gear, as it were, or a lengthening of stride. Whatever the consequences of the change it is hardly fortuitous that it should coincide with the appearance of this first mainspring of the play. The circumstances of the change back to couplets in the final scene is inversely similar. The King has hailed the miraculous restoration of his wealth, has released the Preudom and has accepted Christianity. The main action is complete and what follows is the conversion of the Emirs and the destruction of Tervagant. This phase of the action, although by no means a true anticlimax, is of secondary dramatic interest and being also more popular in tone provides some measure of relief from the more serious and literary tone of the main events of the outcome of the miracle and serves to relax the dramatic tension of the climax. This effect of declaration or, to continue the metaphor, this changing into a lower gear, is well matched by the change from sextets to couplets.

Despite his consistent adherence to these principles of versification, Bodel does not allow them to hamper the natural flow of the dialogue. On the contrary he stimulates its easy flow by frequently dividing rhyming couplets, both independent and within sextets, between speakers. Most of the scenes in couplets show this feature (vss. 121-122, 125-126, 133-134, etc.). Sextets are frequently divided 3 and 3 between speakers, which involves no *réplique par la rime* (vss. 183-188, 189-194, 195-200, etc.), but also their lines are often divided 4 and 2 (vss. 201-206, 333-338, 349-354, etc.), 1 and 5 (vss. 213-218, 361-366, 544-549, etc.), which does involve this linking feature. In addition, many less numerous divisions of the a a b c c b sextet, 2, 3, 1 (vss. 219-224), 1, 2, 1, 2 (vss. 514-519), 3, 1, 2 (vss. 1013-1018), 1, 4, 1 (vss. 1193-1198) and 1, 2, 3 (vss. 1235-1240) also follow this practice. The division of 3, 2, 1, encountered only twice (vss. 538-543 and 1001-1006), is the sole exception but should probably be considered as a variant of the 3 and 3 division in which two sets of lines are linked by the rhyme of the third and sixth lines of the sextet. The alexandrine passages (vss. 239-250, 384-411, and 424-427) show the same freedom in their application to dialogue. As a final observation on Bodel's versification notice should be taken of the further device to ensure the natural flavor of the dialogue, the internal division of lines between speakers (vss. 256, 258, 266, etc.).

## CHAPTER VII

### St. Nicholas

Jean Bodel's reconstruction of the *Iconia* legend of St. Nicholas and his skillful use of crusading and low-life themes culminate in an artistically conceived drama, technically well developed, capturing vividly the spirit of the author's place and time. As a miracle play, however, it is more than a well constructed *pièce de théâtre*; it is an act of faith,[1] an inspired apology of St. Nicholas on the occasion of the celebration of his feast.

St. Nicholas appears in the *Jeu* not merely as a miracle worker but as a saint of God,[2] whose name is throughout the play closely linked with His. Thus the Angel enjoins upon the Preudom: " Soies biens creans ens ou vrai Sauveour / Et en saint Nicolai " (vss. 551-552), and the Preudom likewise counsels the King to give himself " A Dieu, qu'il ait de toi pitié, / Et au baron saint Nicolai " (vss. 1457-1458). Although the *Iconia* legend illustrates the power of the saint as a protector of treasure, it is, as we have noted, not this aspect of his powers which seems to have impressed Bodel most. St. Nicholas' most important rôle is that of the helper of the true believer who has fallen into distress, as here the Preudom. The Preudom's first prayer after his capture is to the saint as " Bons amis Dieu, vrai conseilliere " (vs. 485). When commanded by the King to explain his " mahomet cornu " he says: " Sire, chou est sains Nicolais / Qui les desconsilliés secourt " (vss. 518-519). Finally, when the saint appears to the robbers, he says of himself: " Vassal, je sui sains Nicolais / Qui les desconseilliés ravoie " (vss. 1292-1293). The aspect of the protection of treasure, although essential to the development of the intrigue, occupies a strangely unemphatic position in the prayers to the saint and in the description of his powers. We noticed earlier how the saint's

---

[1] Cf. Petit de Julleville, *Mystères*, I, 190, speaking of the *mystère*: " Or qu'est-ce, à l'origine, que le mystère dramatique, sinon un office, du moins un prolongement, une extension de l'office? Même après qu'il s'en détacha, qu'il sortit de l'Eglise et passa en des mains laïques, le mystère ne perdit jamais tout à fait . . . le caractère religieux qu'il tenait de ses origines."

[2] See Foulon, *Mélanges Cohen*, p. 63.

intervention seems to have as its principal motive the rescue of the Preudom³ and, in examining the Preudom's claims before the King, that the specific claim that St. Nicholas would protect the palace full of treasure seems to be almost an afterthought, merely a concrete illustration of his power in general, added in desperation by the Preudom in an attempt to impress the King.⁴ Herein also lies the explanation of the inconsistency between the Prologue and the play concerning the nature of the restoration of the stolen treasure. In the former the emphasis is on the increase of the returned wealth; in the latter we are concerned with its simple restoration, the only indication at variance with this being in the Seneschal's report after the miracle that it is " Plus grans que il ne fust emblés : / Che m'est avis qu'il est doublés " (vss. 1398-1399). The miracle of the intervention of St. Nicholas in the *Jeu*, then, is more complex and more spiritually elevating than in the traditional legend and in the other versions, emphasizing as it does divine compassion and the Christian concept of succor of the weak and lost. It was in complete neglect of this that Gaston Paris declared: " La simplicité grossière du miracle est plutôt augmentée qu'atténuée dans la pièce de Bodel." ⁵

Believing that the interest of Bodel's play lay elsewhere than in the miraculous intervention of St. Nicholas and not wishing to attach too much importance to the increased " simplicité grossière," the same eminent critic adds: " Mais en somme saint Nicolas apparaît à peine." Yet it is precisely from his single appearance that the saint's " character " draws its greatest strength. As a " bons amis Dieu " he is far above earthly rank. The several messages from Heaven to the knights and to the Preudom are borne by the Angel. To endow the saint with the function of an emissary would be to demean him. To him is reserved the one climactic appearance, instantly solving the several crises of the situation. We are not, however, unprepared for this. The prayers of the Preudom and the words of the Angel constantly and with increasing insistence impress upon us the unseen presence of the saint watching the affairs of men and waiting, as it were, for the moment when his intervention becomes imperative and the most fruitful.

By comparison with the saint of the earlier plays and other

³ See p. 21.
⁴ See p. 89.
⁵ Gaston Paris, *Littérature*, pp. 240-241.

versions of the legend, the St. Nicholas portrayed by Bodel is invested with greater nobility and spiritual worth. As first Rohnstroem [6] and most recently Foulon [7] have pointed out, the saint is impelled to intervene not because his statue has been ill-treated nor for fear of further and more violent reprisals but to save his faithful servant. These critics would go farther and see the saint motivated also by the necessity for defending the Christian faith and by the desire to convert a Saracen people. These, however, would seem to be corollaries to the saving of the truly helpless Christian, which remains the essential act illustrative of the saint's personality.

The comic element of the *Jeu*, covering the whole range of humor of character and action from light satire to sheer buffoonery, does not detract from the new aura of dignity and spiritual worth gracing the figure of St. Nicholas. On the contrary, by its nature and by the place it occupies in the play, it serves to enhance by contrast the elevated tone of the saint's action and the nobility of his character. In considering this aspect of the *Jeu*, it is enlightening to draw a comparison with Hilarius' *Ludus Super Iconia Sancti Nicolai*, representing an earlier phase in the development of the secular from the liturgical drama.[8] Petit de Julleville characterizes Hilarius' humor as *esprit gaulois*: " Ne parlons pas ici de foi naïve, et d'heureuse simplicité. N'alléguons pas la candeur des vieux temps; à toute époque, et même au XII$^e$ siècle, une page telle que celle que nous venons d'analyser, a toujours renfermé une intention légèrement satirique ou du moins ironique. Un demi-sourire s'y dissimule et s'y sous-entend. Ce n'est pas l'incrédulité ouverte et violente, il s'en faut de beaucoup; mais c'est une manière assez gauloise, ou assez française, de rire avec les choses saintes, même en croyant aux Saints. . . . On peut dire qu'avec Hilarius le drame liturgique cesse même d'être religieux." [9] Those who perform the

---

[6] Rohnstroem, pp. 60-61.

[7] Foulon, *Mélanges Cohen*, p. 63.

[8] In his introduction to his edition of the *Jeu*, Jeanroy says of Hilarius' drama: " Ce petit drame est doublement intéressant: d'abord par les intentions comiques qui y apparaissent très nettement et plus encore par la présence, dans les morceaux lyriques, de refrains en français. Il nous achemine donc vers le miracle en langue vulgaire, dont il est fort probable que Bodel n'est pas le créateur " (p. vii).

[9] Petit de Julleville, *Mystères*, I, 74.

play would, accordingly, indulge to some extent at least in the buffoonery latent in the angry *Barbarus'* flogging of the image of the saint.[10] Young does not agree with Petit de Julleville that the *Ludus* is irreligious. The earnestness of the final speech of the *Barbarus*, after his conversion to Christianity, contributes, he contends, a " pleasant elevation of tone." [11] He admits, however, that the French critic was " justly impressed by the suggestion of *esprit gaulois* in the theme and treatment of the piece." [12] The view that this representation of the legend, featuring the fury of the *Barbarus* and the beating of the image of St. Nicholas, is humorous remains unchallenged. The implication that St. Nicholas is moved to intervéne because *he* (through the image) was beaten, embroils him in the grotesque humor of the *Barbarus'* action and detracts from his saintly character.

The comic aspect of the *Jeu* is entirely different. The events closely connected with the miracle are devoid of all suspicion of humor and the character of the saint is in no way impugned. This stems from the important changes stressed earlier concerning the image, made possible by the introduction of the Preudom. The image, endowed with the sanctity of the saint both as a symbol and as the substitute for the saint possessing his miraculous powers of protecting treasure, is not ill-treated. It is against the Preudom that the pagan takes reprisals, and the Preudom, being human, does not appear in an undignified light but as a martyr. The image not being the object of grotesque abuse, the saint himself is not indirectly subjected to indignity and his intervention, made possible by the existence of the Preudom, is dictated, as we have noted, by the highest motives.

The high spiritual purpose and sobriety of the Christian knights needs no further demonstration; neither is the rôle of the Angel in any way humorous. The humorous characters are to be found among the figures of the Saracen court and the tavern; the inherently comic situations of the play involve only these persons; finally, through these characters and situations, Bodel never betrays disrespect for the Church. The proprieties in these respects are perfectly observed and show none of the *esprit gaulois* that Petit de Julleville discerned in Hilarius' play.

[10] Warne, p. xiii.
[11] Young, *Drama*, II, 343.
[12] *Ibid.*

We have had occasion to mention the grotesque irascibility of the King and the humor of the opening scene of the play in which his violent abuse of Tervagant quickly turns to groveling abjectness; we have also noticed the comedy of the interpretation of the oracle by the crafty Seneschal. It is the Saracen religion which is broadly attacked, here and in the final scene showing Tervagant's downfall, not only in the King's, and ultimately the Seneschal's attitude toward the idol, but in such humorous slights of the Saracen faith as the Seneschal's refusal to accept the King's oath sworn by all his gods:

> Sire, bien vous croi seur les diex.
> Mais assés vous querroie miex
> Se vous l'ongle hurtiés au dent.   (vss. 198-200)

Tervagant more than replaces the image of Hilarius' play in providing an object for the type of amusement aroused in that play by the flogging of the image by the *Barbarus*. Grotesque in appearance, submitting to insults and threats, expressing ridiculous anger in a stream of nonsensical sounds (vss. 1517-1520),[13] and ultimately subjected to the indignity of being hurled from his once honored place, he undoubtedly provided the opportunity for much clowning on the stage. The Emirs, too, have a comical aspect. In their boastful bloodthirstiness, in their wealth and pomp, or, as in the case of Sec Arbre, the exaggerated lack of it, and in their servile obedience to their ignoble King, they resemble brightly colored puppets, ridiculous in movement and appearance. The nature of their conversion, a blind following of the example of the King by three of them, and the highly insulting refusal to acquiesce on the part of Orkenie, compelled, however, to abjure his faith in a most undignified manner, completes their comic characterization. Auberon, impudent in his efficiency and smartly outwitting the Tavernkeeper in the way he avoids paying for his drink at the inn, stands in amusing contrast to the other minor official of the King's household, Connart. Staid and pompous and jealously proud of his duties, he provides, with Raoulet, the amusing spectacle of the quarrel over the crying of the wine. The comment in an earlier chapter on the comic personalities and actions of the characters of the tavern, the Tavernkeeper, Caignet, and the

---

[13] Cf. the words of Salatin in conjuring up the Devil in Rutebeuf's *Miracle de Théophile*, ed. G. Frank, CFMA (Paris, 1925), vss. 160-168.

thieves, Cliquet, Pincedé, and Rasoir, an aptly and amusingly named trio, needs no elaboration. Suffice it to say that whereas the comedy of the scenes of the Saracen court is grotesque, the tavern scenes provide the earthy, familiar, realistic humor of Arras low-life, yet never sinking to the excessive indecency of the contemporary *fabliau*.

Despite the careful separation of the comic and serious scenes and the absence of satirical and disrespectful comment on Christian matters, the introduction of humorous elements in a serious miracle play would strike a modern audience as objectionable. Yet in his drama of St. Nicholas, Bodel was following an old tradition. From the earliest times the comic element had its place in the lives of the saints. In his treatment of the subject, Curtius [14] shows that not only in literature devoted to the martyrdom of the saints is there a comic element in the surprising behavior of holy figures towards their tormentors [15] (this is explained as a deliberate attempt on the part of the victim to seek even more violent torture and to increase his martyrdom), but that also in the *vitae* is humor often present. Thus, in the prose life of St. Martin by Sulpicius Severus,[16] there is an element of comedy in the treatment of the incident of the advancing heathen being halted by the saint; unable to move forward " ridiculam in vertiginem rotabantur " (pp. 122, 8). Later versions of this same *vita* show other incidents cast in a humorous light. Paulinus of Périgeux [17] introduces a note of levity in describing the sudden inability of the saint's would-be executioner to move his arm, uplifted to strike off with the sword his victim's head, obligingly thrust out (2, 451). Again, in the ver-

---

[14] Curtius, " Hagiographische Komik," *Europäische Literatur*, pp. 426-430.

[15] E. g., Eulalia:

> Martyr ad ista nihil, sed enim
> Infremit inque tyranni oculos
> Sputa iacit.
> (Prudentius, *Peristephanon*, vss. 126-128)

R. Menéndez Pidal, *Historia de la España* (Madrid, 1935), II, xxix, refers to this as the " infantil discomedimiento de Eulalia." He also speaks of the " humorismo atroz de Lorenzo en el suplicio."

[16] *Sulpicii Severi Opera*, ed. C. Halm, CSEL, I (Vienna, 1866), pp. 109-137.

[17] *Poetae Christiani minores*, CSEL, XVI (Vienna, Prague, and Leipzig, 1888), Part I, 19-159.

sion of Fortunatus, the Devil, in the guise now of Mercury, now of Jupiter, is made to look ridiculous. These are typical instances of heathens, the Devil, and the wicked being ridiculed. The Carolingian period offers many examples of this. Einhard describes with comic effect the trial of strength of Peter the Exorcist and his jailer.[18] In the life of St. Germanus by Heiricus the saint tracks down a horse-thief,[19] and the Devil complains of the narrowing down of his sphere of action.[20] Sometimes the poet himself directly pours scorn on the Devil, as does Milo in his Life of St. Amandus.[21] In the story of the martyrdom of St. Christopher, the saint resists the advances of two women who attempt to seduce him; converted to Christianity, they return to their king to tell him his idols are worthless.[22] Finally, in the Life of St. Amandus again, a humorous castigation of a *mimus* is given.[23] Such was the long tradition of the existence of comic elements in hagiographic literature. By Bodel's time the public had come to expect such treatment of stories of the saints, seeing in it not a sign of disrespect but, in the ridiculing of the saint's adversaries and of behavior that conflicted with the saintly life, an emphasis on the virtues and superior powers of the saint.

The crux of the answer to those who speak of incongruities in the *Jeu*, the juxtaposition of lofty and low, spiritual and material, exotic and familiar, serious and comic, lies then in the attitude of the common man of the medieval city to his saints. " Bons amis Dieu " and among the most highly venerated of saints, St. Nicholas was, nevertheless, essentially the saint of the humble and lowly. He was the hope in times of greatest trouble and a constant source of comfort in daily prayer and, as an integral part in the pattern of the man's daily troubled existence, he was always seen with familiar eyes. This single key to the appreciation of the *Jeu de saint Nicolas* was, ironically enough, in the hands of the critic most to disparage the spiritual values of the play. Petit de Julle-

---

[18] " Passio Marcellini et Petri," *Poetae latini aevi Carolini*, MGH (Berlin, 1881-1937), II, 128, 21.

[19] *Poetae*, III, 481, 229 ff.

[20] *Poetae*, III, 496, 291 ff.

[21] *Poetae*, III, 583, 191 ff.

[22] *Poetae*, IV, 822, 152 ff.

[23] *Poetae*, III, 600.

ville might well have applied to the *Jeu* the striking lesson of his own appreciation of the attitude of medieval man to his saints:

Les hommes du XII<sup>e</sup> siècle voyaient les saints d'autres yeux que les plus croyants ne les voient aujourd'hui. Ils les sentaient plus près d'eux, pour ainsi dire, et leur vénération, pour être singulièrement plus enthousiaste, n'en était pas moins plus familière, leur vision plus immédiate, leur confiance plus abandonnée. Ni la sainteté ni le miracle ne les étonnent; et quand ils posent le pied sur le terrain des vertus ou des faits surnaturels, ils se croient encore chez eux.[24]

---

[24] Petit de Julleville, *Histoire de la langue et de la littérature française* (Paris, 1896), I, 1, 22-23.

# BIBLIOGRAPHY

Adams, J. Q., ed. Chief Pre-Shakespearean Dramas. Boston and New York, 1924.
Albrecht, O. E., ed. Four Latin plays of St. Nicholas from the twelfth century Fleury play-book. Philadelphia, 1935.
Andolf, Sven, ed. Floovant, chanson de geste du XIIe siècle, publiée avec introduction, notes et glossaire, thèse pour le doctorat. Uppsala, 1941.
Anrich, G. Hagios Nikolaos, der heilige Nickolaos in der griechischen Kirche. Leipzig, 1913-1917. Vol. I.
Bédier, Joseph, ed. La chanson de Roland. Publiée d'après le manuscript d'Oxford et traduite. Paris, 1922. 2 vols.
Brandin, Louis, ed. La chanson d'Aspremont, chanson de geste du XIIe siècle, texte du manuscrit de Wollaton Hall. CFMA. Paris, 1919. 2 vols.
Brunel, C. Review of A. Jeanroy's " Jean Bodel, trouvère artésien du XIIIe siècle: le Jeu de saint Nicolas." BEC, LXXXVII (1926), 407-408.
Carnahan, D. H. The Prologue in the Old French and Provençal Mystery. New Haven, 1905.
Champollion-Figeac, J. J., ed. Hilarii Versus et Ludi. Paris, 1838.
Clédat, L. Rutebeuf. Paris, 1891.
———. Sur un dicton auxerrois du XIIIe siècle. RLR, XXII (1882), 99-101.
Comfort, W. W. The literary rôle of the Saracens in the French Epic. PMLA, LV (1940), 628-659.
———. The character types in the Old French *chansons de geste*. PMLA, XXI (1906), 279-432.
Cousins, C. E. Deux parties de dés dans le " Jeu de saint Nicolas." Rom., LVII (1931), 436-437.
———. Tavern bills in the " Jeu de saint Nicolas." ZRP, LVI (1936), 85-93.
de Coussemaker, E., ed. Drames liturgiques du moyen âge. Rennes, 1860.
Crawford, M. S., ed. Life of St. Nicholas. University of Pennsylvania dissertation. Philadelphia, 1924.
Crosland, Jessie. The Old French epic. Oxford, 1951.
Curtius, E. R. Europäische Literatur und lateinisches Mittelalter. Bern, 1948.
Delahaye, H. Les légendes hagiographiques. RQH, nouvelle série, XXX (1903), 56-122.
Del Valle de Paz, Ida. La leggenda di S. Nicola nella tradizione poetica medioevale in Francia. Florence, 1921.
Delius, N., ed. Maistre Wace's St. Nicholas, ein altfranzösisches Gedicht des zwölften Jahrhunderts aus Oxforder Handschriften. Bonn, 1850.

Dickman, Adolphe Jacques. Le rôle du surnaturel dans les chansons de geste, thèse de doctorat. Iowa, 1925.

Dinaux, A. Trouvères, jongleurs et ménestrels du Nord de la France. III, Les trouvères artésiens. Paris and Valenciennes, 1843.

Dubois, M. Sur un passage obscur du "Jeu de saint Nicholas." Rom., LV (1929), 256-258.

Du Méril, E. Les origines latines du théâtre moderne. Paris, 1849; facsimile reproduction Leipzig and Paris, 1897.

Falconius, N. C., ed. Sancti Confessoris Pontificis et celeberrimi thaumaturgi Nicolai Acta Primigenia. Naples, 1751.

Faral, E., ed. Courtois d'Arras, jeu du XIII<sup>e</sup> siècle. 2nd ed. rev. CFMA. Paris, 1922.

Fissen, K. Das Leben des heiligen Nikolaus in der altfranzösichen Literatur und seine Quellen. Dissertation, Göttingen, 1921.

Foulet, L. Les scènes de taverne dans le "Jeu de saint Nicolas." Rom., LXVIII (1944-45), 425-438.

Foulon, C. Les comptes du tavernier dans le "Jeu de saint Nicolas." Rom., LXVIII (1944-45), 438-443.

———. La représentation et sources du "Jeu de saint Nicolas." Mélanges d'histoire du théâtre du moyen âge et de la renaissance offerts à Gustave Cohen. Paris, 1950, pp. 54-106.

Frank, G. Review of F. J. Warne's "Jean Bodel: le Jeu de saint Nicolas." RR, XLII (Dec. 1951), 282-284.

———, ed. Rutebeuf: le miracle de Théophile. CFMA. Paris, 1925.

———. Wine reckonings in Bodel's "Jeu de saint Nicolas." MLN, 50 (1935), 9-13.

Fuller, J. B. Hilarii versus et ludi, edited from the Paris manuscript. New York, 1929.

Gill, A. A note on the gamblers' quarrels in the "Jeu de saint Nicolas." Med. A., VIII (1939), 50-53.

Gougenheim, G., ed. Cortebarbe: les trois aveugles de Compiègne, fabliau du XIII<sup>e</sup> siècle. CFMA. Paris, 1932.

Graesse, T., ed. Jacobus a Voragine, Legenda aurea vulgo historia lombardica dicta. Dresden and Leipzig, 1846.

Guesnon, A. Trouvères artésiens. MA, XXI (1908), 67-86.

Halm, C., ed. Sulpicii Severi Opera. CSEL, I. Vienna, 1866.

Hatem, Anouar. Les poèmes épiques des Croisades, thèse pour le doctorat d'université. Paris, 1932.

Hilka, A. Review of A. Jeanroy's "Jean Bodel, trouvère artésien du XIII<sup>e</sup> siècle: le Jeu de saint Nicolas." ZRP, XLVI (1926) 492.

Jeanroy, A., ed. Jean Bodel, trouvère artésien du XIII<sup>e</sup> siècle: le Jeu de saint Nicolas. CFMA. Paris, 1925.

———. Réminiscences de "Fierabras" dans le "Jeu de saint Nicolas." Rom., L (1924), 435-438.

Jubinal Achille, ed. Nouveau recueil de contes, dits, fabliaux et autres pièces inédites des XIII<sup>e</sup>, XIV<sup>e</sup> et XV<sup>e</sup> siècles. Paris, 1839. Vol. I.

Knudson, C. A. Hasard et les autres jeux de dés dans le "Jeu de saint Nicolas." Rom., LXIII (1937), 248-253.

Kroeber, A., and Servois, G., eds. Fierabras, chanson de geste publiée pour la première fois d'après les manuscrits de Paris, de Rome et de Londres. APF. Paris, 1860.

Langlois, E., ed. Le couronnement de Louis, chanson de geste du XII<sup>e</sup> siècle. CFMA. Paris, 1920.

Le Grand d'Aussy, P. J.-B., ed. Fabliaux ou contes du XII<sup>e</sup> et du XIII<sup>e</sup> siècle. Paris, 1779. Vol. I.

Le Roy, O. Etudes sur les mystères. Paris, 1837.

Lintilhac, E. Le théâtre sérieux du moyen âge. Paris, 1904.

des Longrais, F. Joüon, ed. Le Roman d'Aquin ou la conqueste de la Bretaigne par le roy Charlemaigne, chanson de geste du XII<sup>e</sup> siècle. SBB. Nantes, 1880.

McMillan, D., ed. La chanson de Guillaume. SATF. Paris, 1949. 2 vols.

———. Review of F. J. Warne's "Jean Bodel: le Jeu de saint Nicolas." MLR, XLVII (April, 1952), 237-240.

Mâle, E. L'Art religieux du XIII<sup>e</sup> siècle en France. Paris, 1925.

Manly, J. M. Literary forms and the new theory of the origin of species. MP, IV (1906-7), 577-595.

Manz, G. Li jus de saint Nicolas des Arrasers Jean Bodel. Text mit eine Untersuchung der Sprache und des Metrums des Stückes, nebst Anmerkungen und Glossar. Heidelberg dissertation. Erlangen, 1904.

Meisen, K. Nikolauskult und Nikolasbrauch im Abendlande, eine kultgeographisch-volkskundliche Untersuchung. Forschungen zur Volkskunde IX-XII. Duesseldorf, 1931.

Menéndez Pidal, R. Historia de la España. Madrid, 1935. II.

Meyer, P. De l'allitération en roman de France, à propos d'une formule allitérée relative aux qualités du vin. Rom., XI (1882), 572-579.

Mombritius, Boninus, ed. Sanctuarium seu Vitae Sanctorum. Milan, 1479; reprinted: Sanctuarium seu Vitae Sanctorum, novam hanc Editionem curaverunt duo Monachi solesmenses. Paris, 1910. Vol. II.

Monmerqué, L.-J.-N. Mélanges publiés pour la Société des Bibliophiles français: VII. Paris, 1834.

———, et Michel, F., eds. Théâtre français au moyen âge. Paris, 1839.

Montaiglon, A. de, and Raynaud, G., eds. Recueil général et complet des fabliaux du XIII<sup>e</sup> et du XIV<sup>e</sup> siècle. Librairie des bibliophiles. Paris, 1872-90. 6 vols.

Paris, Gaston. Histoire poétique de Charlemagne. Paris, 1905.

———. La Légende de Pépin 'le Bref.' Mélanges de littérature française du moyen âge. Published by Mario Roques. Paris, 1912, pp. 103-215.

———. La littérature française au moyen âge. Paris, 1888.

Perrier, J. L., ed. Le siège de Barbastre, chanson de geste du XII<sup>e</sup> siècle. CFMA. Paris, 1926.

Petit de Julleville, L. Histoire de la langue et de la littérature française. Paris, 1896. Vol. I.

———. Les Mystères. Paris, 1880. 2 vols.

Poetae Christiani minores. CSEL, XVI. Vienna, Prague and Leipzig, 1888.

Poetae latini aevi Carolini. MGH. Berlin, 1881-1937. 5 vols.

Pollard, A. W., ed. English miracle plays, moralities and interludes. Oxford, 1923.
Raynaud, G., ed. Les congés de Jean Bodel. Rom., IX (1880), 217-247. Reprinted in Mélanges de philologie romane. Paris, 1913, pp. 276-314.
Robert de Clari. La conquête de Constantinople. ed. Phillippe Lauer. CFMA. Paris, 1924.
Rohnstroem. Etude sur Jean Bodel. Thèse pour le doctorat. Uppsala, 1900.
Ronsjö, Einar, ed. La Vie de saint Nicolas par Wace. Lund, 1942.
Roques, Mario. Pour le commentaire " d'Aucassin et Nicolette " ' esclairier le cuer.' Mélanges l'histoire du moyen âge offerts à M. Ferdinand Lot. Paris, 1925. Pp. 723-736.
Sainéan, L. Les sources indigènes de l'etymologie française. Paris, 1925. 2 vols.
Schulze, A. Review of G. Manz' " Li jus de saint Nicholas des Arrasers Jean Bodel." ZRP, XXX (1906), 102-108.
Semrau, F. Würfel und Würfelspiel im alten Frankreich. Beiheft zur ZRP, XXIII (1910).
Sepet, Marius. Origines catholiques du théâtre moderne. Paris, 1901.
Spitzer, L. Etudes d'anthroponymie ancienne française. II. Pépin ' le Bref.' PMLA, LVII (1943), 593-596.
———. The Prologue to the " Lais " of Marie de France and Medieval Poetics. MP, XLI (1943), 96-102.
Spitzer, R. Beiträge zur Geschichte des Spiels in Alt-Frankreich. Diss. Heidelberg, 1891.
Terracher, A.-L., ed. La chevalerie Vivien, chanson de geste. Paris, 1909.
Villehardhouin, G. de. La conquête de Constantinople. Ed. and trans. E. Faral. Paris, 1938. 2 vols.
Vincent de Beauvais. Speculum historiale. Strasburg, 1473. 4 vols.
Wallensköld, A. Review of A. Jeanroy's " Jean Bodel, trouvère artésien du XIIIe siècle: le Jeu de saint Nicolas." NM, XXVII (1926), 176.
Warne, F. J., ed. Jean Bodel: le Jeu de saint Nicolas. Blackwell's French Texts. Oxford, 1951.
Wright, T., ed. Early mysteries and other Latin poems of the twelfth and thirteenth centuries. London, 1838.
———, and Halliwell, J. O. Reliquiae antiquae. Scraps from ancient manuscripts, illustrating early English literature and the English language. London, 1843. 2 vols.
Young, Karl. The drama of the medieval Church. Oxford, 1933. 2 vols.

# ABBREVIATIONS

| | |
|---|---|
| APF: | Anciens poètes de la France |
| BEC: | Bibliothèque de l'Ecole des Chartes |
| CFMA: | Les classiques français du moyen âge |
| CSEL: | Corpus Scriptorum Ecclesiasticorum Latinorum |
| MA: | Moyen âge |
| Med. A: | Medium Aevum |
| MGH: | Monumenta Germaniae Historica |
| MLN: | Modern Language Notes |
| MLR: | Modern Language Review |
| MP: | Modern Philology |
| NM: | Neuphilologische Mitteilungen |
| PL: | Patrologia Latina |
| RLR: | Revue des langues romanes |
| Rom. | Romania |
| RQH: | Revue des questions historiques |
| RR: | Romanic Review |
| SATF: | Société des anciens textes français |
| SBB: | Société des bibliophiles bretons |
| ZRP: | Zeitschrift für romanische philologie |

# INDEX

*Only the most significant mentions of the characters of the play referred to throughout the study are given in the index.*

Arica, King of, 57–60
Agolant, King of the Saracens, 47–52 *passim*, 62–63
Aigremont, 49
Albrecht, Otto, 26 n, 31 n
Alexander the Great, 54 n
Alfonso X of Castille, 76
*Aliscans*, 43
Amauri of Berry, 49
Angel, the, 48
Anseïs of Cologne, 55
Antelme of Tours, 49
Apolin, 57, 59, 60
*Aquin*, 46
Archamp, 43–51 *passim*
Arras, *passim*
Aspremont, 47–63 *passim*
Athon, 51
Auberon, 54–57, 68–70
Augier, 61
Auxerre, 31, 33, 78, 79

Balan, 49–62 *passim*
Baligant, 48, 62
Barbarus (Diaconus), 18
Barbarus (Hilarius), 25–26, 27, 100, 101
Bari, Apulia, 31
Baud, 64
Baudouin IX of Flanders, 64
Bodel, Jean, *passim*
—*Les Congés (Congiés)*, 10, 64
—*Chanson de Saisnes*, 41
Bourges, 31
Brittany, 46
Bruges, 64
Brulans, 58
Brunols of Hungary, 55

Cahoër of England, 55
Cahu, 57
Caignet, 73-75
Calabria, 17, 18, 47, 51
*Chanson de Guillaume*, 43, 50–51
*Chanson de Roland*, 7, 41–62 *passim*
Charlemagne, 42 n, 46–58 *passim*, 84
Chartres, 31, 33
*Chevalerie Vivien*, 46, 51
Claire, 63
Clédat, Léon, 13 n
Cliquet, 67–82 *passim*
Coine, Emir of, 55–56
Connart, 80–81
Cordova, Governor of, 59
Cordroés, 58
Corsolt, 53
Cortebarbe
—*Des trois avugles de Compiègne*, 69
*Couronnement de Louis*, 47–53 *passim*
*Courtois d'Arras*, 69, 79
Crestïens nouviaus chevaliers, 48-53
Curtius, Ernst Robert, 53 n, 101-103

David and Goliath, 54 n
David of Cornwall, 55
Del Valle de Paz, Ida, 13–14 n
*Desputoison du vin et de l'iaue*, 78, 79
Descramé, 43, 46, 50
Devil, the, 103
Diaconus, Johannes, of Naples, 17
—*Iconia Sancti Nicolai*, 17–25, 27, 30, 33, 35
Dol, Archbishop of, 46

Droon of Manseis (Mansois), 55–56
Durant, 82

Eaumont, 47, 49, 52
Einhard, 103
Estolt, 51
Eulalia, 102 n

Falconius, N. C., 17
Fierabras, 53, 61, 62
*Fierabras*, 41–42, 48–63 *passim*
Fleury manuscript, the, 6, 6 n, 9, 25–30
*Floovant*, 57
Floripas, 61
Fortunatus, 103
Foulon, Charles, 32 n, 99
Foulque de Neuilly, 10, 64
Fourth Crusade, 10, 64, 65
Fraisne, 82

Gabriel, 48
Gaians, 54
Gaverele, 82
Girard (Girars) d'Eufrate, 47, 62
Godefroi de Boulogne, 49
Gondelbuef the Frisian, 55
Guesnon, A., 68 n
Gui, 50–51
Guiborc, 50, 51
Guichardés, 50, 51
Guion, 51

Heiricus, 103
Henin, 81
Herod, 58 n
Hilarius
—*Ludus super iconia sancti Nicolai*, 6, 6 n, 9, 25–30, 99, 100, 101
Honorius of Autun, 32
*Huon de Bordeaux*, 41

Innocent III, Pope, 10, 64

Jacobus de Voragine. *See Legenda aurea*
Jeanroy, Alfred, 13, 41–63 *passim*, 94 n, 99 n

Jew, the, 26, 33, 34
Jupiter, 57, 103

Knudson, Charles A., 75–76

Laon, 51
La Vallière, duc de, 3
*Legenda aurea*, 9, 32
Legendaries, North and South English and Scottish, 33
Le Grand d'Aussy, Pierre J.-B., 3–4
Le Mans, 31, 33
Lequet, 79
LeRoy, Onésime, 4–6, 7–11 *passim*, 40, 49, 83
Louis the Pious, 60
Louis IX. *See* St. Louis
Lintilhac, Eugène, 13n, 83

Mahomet (Mahom), 52–62 *passim*
Mâle, Emile, 30–31
Mandaquin, 53
Mansoura, 5
Margot, 57
Marsilie, 60
Menéndez Pidal, Ramon, 102 n
Mercury, 48, 103
Methodius, Patriarch of Constantinople, 17
Methodius ad Honorem, 17
Michael the Archimandrite, 17
Milo, 103
Mombritius, Boninus, 17
Myra, Asia Minor, 31

Naimes, Duke of, 47, 49–50, 52
Nicholas, Bishop of Myra, 9, 16
Nicoles li Carpentiers, 64

Ogier le Danois, 52
Oliferne, Emir of, 55–56
Oliver, 43–62 *passim*
Orkenie, Emir of, 55–56, 61–63
Outre le Sec Arbre, Emir of, 55–57

Paris, Gaston, 13 n, 54 n, 83-84, 98
Pépin le Bref, 54 n
Peter Damian, 32

# INDEX

Peter the Exorcist, 103
Petit de Julleville, L., 5–8, 10, 11, 13 n, 25, 83, 97 n, 99–100, 103-104
Pincedé, 67–82 *passim*
Pourette, 79
Preecierces, the, 15, 16, 24
Preudom, the, 20–22

Queneliex, 54

Raoulet, 80–81
Rasoir, 67–77 *passim*
Reims, 31
Renaut de Bieauvais, 64
Richard Cœur de Lion, 10
Richier, 49
Robert, Count of Artois, 5
Robert de Clari, 64
Robert Piedargentionis, 64
Rohnstroem, Otto, 7n, 8–13, 26n, 83, 94n, 99
Roland, 48–53 *passim*
Romantics, the, 8
Roncevaux, 43, 45
Ronsjö, Einar, 16n, 31n
Rouen, 31, 33
Rutebuef
—*Le miracle de Théophile*, 3n, 101n

Saladin, 10
Salatin, 101 n
Saracens, *passim*
Soleman, King of the Bretons, 49, 52, 55
St. Amandus, 103
St. Benoît, 68
Saint-Benoît-sur-Loire, 6 n
St. Bernard of Clairvaux, 32
St. Christopher, 103
St. Dominique, 48
St. George, 48, 53
St. Germanus, 103
St. James of Compostella, 31
Saint-Julien-du-Sault, 31, 33
St. Lawrence, 102 n
St. Louis (Louis IX), 4–5, 7 n

St. Martin of Tours, 30, 31, 102
Saint-Nicolas du Port, 31
St. Nicholas of Sion, 17
Saint-Rémi, 31
Shakespeare, 4, 7, 8
*Siège de Barbastre*, 57, 58–59
Simon Disier, 64
Sortinbras, 58
Spain, Emir of, 59–60
Spitzer, Leo, 38–39 n
Sulpicius Severus, 102

Tavernkeeper, 66–79 *passim*
Tempeste, 58
Tervagant, 57–60
*Thauma de imagine in Africa*, 17
Thelonarius (Diaconus), 18, 20, 22
Thibaut III of Champagne, 64
Third Crusade, 10
Thomas, 64
Tiberias, 10
Tolnoiers (Wace), 19–26 *passim*
Tours, 31, 33
Troyes, 33
Tunis, King of, 5
Turpin, Archbishop, 45

Vandals, 17, 18, 19
Varangueville, 31
Villehardouin, Geoffroi de, 64
Vincent of Beauvais
—Speculum Historiale, 32
Vivien, 43, 46, 50, 51

Waast Hukedeu, 64
Wace
—*Vie de saint Nicolas*, 9, 18–25, 30, 32, 38
Waignet, 64
Wanquetin, 77
Warne, F. J., 13, 26 n, 43, 67, 76 n, 81 n, 92 n, 93 n, 94 n
William of Orange, 43–53 *passim*

Young, Karl, 100

## LIBRARY OF DAVIDSON COLLEGE

Books on regular loan may be checked out for two weeks. must be presented at the Circulation Desk in order

A fine of **five cents** a day is

Special books are subj
of library staff.

MAR 28 1974